W9-AVL-979

CONTENTS

INTRODUCTION 4

CHAPTER ONE
THE POET and THE DREAMER 8

CHAPTER TWO
"GIVE PEACE a CHANCE" 28

CHAPTER THREE
STORY OF an ASSASSIN 40

CHAPTER FOUR
DEATH on THE DOORSTEP 52

CHAPTER FIVE
POSTMORTEM 64

CHAPTER SIX
"STRAWBERRY FIELDS FOREVER" 78

TIMELINE 86
WHO'S WHO? 88
SOURCE NOTES 90
SELECTED BIBLIOGRAPHY 92
FOR FURTHER INFORMATION 92
INDEX 94

INTRODUCTION

AN UNSPEAKABLE TRAGEDY CONFIRMED TO US BY ABC NEWS IN NEW YORK CITY. JOHN LENNON, outside of his apartment building on the west side of New York City, the most famous, perhaps, of all of the Beatles, shot twice in the back, rushed to Roosevelt Hospital, dead on arrival.

—HOWARD COSELL, DECEMBER 8, 1980

A large crowd assembled outside the Dakota, the New York City apartment building where rock icon John Lennon had lived with his wife, Yoko Ono, and their five-year-old son, Sean, since 1973.

Sportscaster Howard Cosell broke into the live television broadcast of *Monday Night Football* as millions of Americans watched and listened in disbelief. In those early moments, some of Cosell's details were wrong, but the most important and devastating fact was true. John Lennon—former member of the legendary rock group the Beatles and one of the most famous people in the world—had been shot and killed. Gunned down late at night outside his home by a lone assassin—Mark David Chapman—Lennon was pronounced dead shortly after reaching Roosevelt Hospital.

Reports of the assassination stunned the world. Fans reacted with shock and grief. Anchorman Walter Cronkite opened the December 9 *CBS Evening News* with,

Police arrested Mark David Chapman within minutes of his shooting John Lennon. This mug shot was taken the next day, December 9, 1980.

away as Hungary, Japan, and Russia—spread the news. In the first hours after Lennon's death, many mourners simply wanted to sing his songs and remember his life. Questions about the man who murdered Lennon came later.

In New York City—which had been John's home for almost a decade—some fans gathered outside Roosevelt Hospital. A larger crowd assembled outside the Dakota, the apartment building where rock icon John Lennon lived with his wife, Yoko Ono, and their five-year-old son, Sean. By four in the morning, a crowd of five hundred people maintained a vigil outside the Dakota. The crowd would later grow to about one thousand.

Cynthia O'Neal, a resident of the Dakota in 1980, was at home when one of her sons heard gunshots outside the building. "We turned on the television and watched the horror [of Lennon's assassination] unfold, terrible detail by terrible detail," she said. O'Neal

"The death of a man who sang and played guitar overshadows the news from Poland, Iran, and Washington tonight." That same night, the U.S. late-night news show *Nightline* focused on Lennon's life and death. Many radio stations set aside their usual schedules to play the music of Lennon and the Beatles. Newspaper headlines around the United States and Great Britain, Lennon's birthplace—and even as far

DEATHLY DEFINITIONS

he dictionary definitions below help clarify what makes an assassination a unique crime.

ASSASSINATE: to murder (a usually prominent person) by sudden or secret attack, often for political reasons
KILL: to deprive of life; cause the death of
MURDER: to kill (a human being) unlawfully and with premeditated malice [intent to do harm]

Lennon's death is generally viewed as an assassination. Chapman singled him out because of the singer's fame and views on religion and politics.

went on to recall the impromptu tribute that followed Lennon's death. "People started arriving outside the building almost immediately. That night was the first of many when I lay in bed, completely awake, eyes wide, listening to the chanting, the mantra, float up from the street below. . . . I found it very comforting. I liked knowing how many other hearts were broken."

For the rest of the night—and for the next several days—brokenhearted fans honored and mourned their hero. With candles in their hands and with tears streaming down their faces, they sang John Lennon's songs into the chilly night air.

CHAPTER ONE

THE **POET**
and THE **DREAMER**

You make your own dream.

—JOHN LENNON, 1980

J ohn Winston Lennon was born to Julia and Alfred Lennon in Liverpool, England, on October 9, 1940. Located on England's northwestern coast, Liverpool is a bustling port city. It has a reputation for toughness but also for humor, culture, and diversity.

Baby John entered a world at war. World War II (1939–1945) had begun when Germany, under Nazi dictator Adolf Hitler, invaded Poland. Other nations joined the fight, falling into two camps. The Axis powers included Germany, Italy, and Japan. The Allies included Great Britain, France, the United States, and the Soviet Union (fifteen republics that included Russia).

On the night of John's birth, a German air raid on Liverpool raged beyond the hospital windows. Julia Lennon's older sister, Mimi Smith, braved the falling rubble to visit the hospital and see her newborn nephew. Mimi later recalled, "Just as I lifted him up, the warning sirens went off again and visitors were told we could either go down into the cellars or go home but we couldn't stay. John, like the other babies, was put under the bed for safety. I ran every step of the way home."

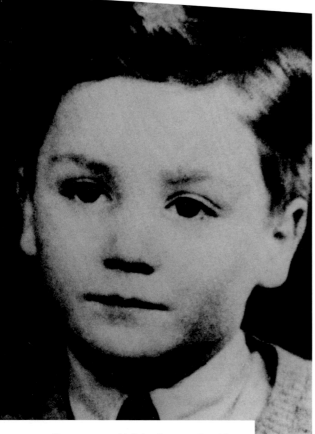

Seven-year-old John Lennon lived in Liverpool, England, in the 1940s.

John's first days were marked by war. His father worked mainly as part of Britain's Merchant Navy on ships carrying troops during the war. This work kept him away from Liverpool most of the time. Young, fun-loving, and not-very-responsible Julia struggled to care for her baby alone. Mimi suggested that she take on most of the responsibility for caring for John, and Julia agreed. By the time he was about five years old, John had moved in with his aunt Mimi and her husband, George Smith. Their Liverpool home, called Mendips, was modest and comfortable. It was also full of love. While Mimi could be strict, she and George adored their little nephew. Julia visited occasionally, but young John's closest family ties were with Mimi and George.

FROM SCHOOLBOY TO QUARRYMAN

Aunt Mimi had her work cut out for her. John was never a model student. After attending Liverpool's Dovedale Primary School, John entered Quarry Bank High School shortly before his twelfth birthday. Things went downhill from there. John was intelligent, but he was also rebellious. He had little patience or respect for authority figures. At Quarry Bank, he taunted teachers, skipped classes, and made trouble. He earned a reputation as a class clown—wisecracking, witty, and disobedient.

A somber event shook John in 1955, however—the sudden death of his beloved uncle George. Afterward, John became even more unsettled. He struggled with his grief and wondered about his future. He thought about dropping out of school without graduating. But his talent in art—and Aunt Mimi's fierce support—eventually won him a place at the Liverpool College of Art.

John enjoyed the visual arts, but a different passion was seizing him. Elvis Presley had burst onto the music scene in the United States with his 1956 song "Heartbreak Hotel." When the bold new sound of Elvis's rock and roll reached England, John was hooked. "After that, nothing was the same for me," John later said.

As soon as John got his hands on a cheap guitar, the home was filled with music. Irritated by John's seemingly constant playing, Mimi would send her nephew to the front porch. The guitar may have annoyed Mimi, but it helped bring John and his mother closer together. Julia played the banjo and taught John a few basic chords (groups of notes played together).

In 1950s England, a musical style called skiffle was hot. Skiffle had originated in the United States in the 1920s. It combined elements of jazz, blues, and folk music. By the 1940s, the skiffle style had

John spent most of his childhood living with his aunt Mimi and uncle George Smith in this home in Liverpool. The home was called Mendips.

Skiffle groups were popular while John was in his teens. These groups played washboards, tea-chest basses, and guitars. Skiffle made music accessible to average people.

mostly fizzled out in the United States. But the 1950s brought a skiffle revival in Great Britain.

A big part of skiffle's appeal was its roughness and accessibility. You didn't have to be a trained musician to play it. All you needed was a guitar—not even a good one—and an assortment of cheap, often homemade instruments. Usually one band member played a washboard by running thimbles over the board's rippled metal surface. Another skiffle staple was the tea-chest bass. This makeshift instrument consisted of a tea chest (a large wooden box), some long string, and a broomstick or pole of some sort. Together, these bits and pieces formed a very basic string bass. Skiffle groups soon sprang up all over British front stoops and school yards. Some music historians estimate that the nation had about thirty to fifty thousand skiffle groups by the late 1950s.

John and his schoolmates were among those thousands. John and several fellow students formed a group called the Quarrymen, after Quarry Bank High School. John's fellow members included his best friend, Pete Shotton, who played the washboard.

On July 6, 1957, the Quarrymen played at a local festival held by Saint Peter's Church in a suburb of Liverpool. A fellow teenager named Paul McCartney was in the audience. McCartney, who came from a musical family, could sing and knew how to play guitar. John soon asked him to join the Quarrymen—and McCartney agreed.

John began attending art college in the autumn of 1957. The habits that had gotten him into trouble at Quarry Bank didn't change much at college. He rebelled against his instructors, neglected his assignments, and sometimes skipped class.

Meanwhile, John's passion for music was growing. McCartney was a student at the nearby Liverpool Institute. Soon George Harrison, another Liverpool Institute student, joined the Quarrymen. John, Paul, and George often met over lunch to make music. They played tunes made famous by their rock-and-roll heroes. Before long, they were writing their own songs and skipping classes to practice.

On July 15, 1958, Julia was hit and killed instantly by a drunk driver. Seventeen-year-old John was devastated by his mother's sudden death. To ease his grief, he sought comfort in music. He, McCartney, and Harrison continued to write and play music. In May 1960, the band—renamed the Silver Beetles—went on a short tour of Scotland. They weren't the tour's headliners. But the experience brought them to a wider

FROM SKIFFLE TO STARDOM

he Beatles were not the only young skifflers who went on to make it big. Other skifflers include the musicians Van Morrison, Mick Jagger of the Rolling Stones, Jimmy Page of Led Zeppelin, Roger Daltrey of the Who, and David Gilmour of Pink Floyd.

audience and gave them a taste of life on the road. In August the band's manager, Allan Williams, landed them a gig (job) playing at a club in Hamburg, Germany.

But first, the band needed a permanent drummer. They asked people in the local music scene for ideas, and heard about Pete Best. Best had played drums with a number of other bands and was well liked. He was also willing to travel to Germany on short notice. The group had themselves a drummer. Renaming themselves the Beatles, the four musicians headed to Germany.

The Beatles pose for a band photo in 1961. **From left:** Paul McCartney, Pete Best, George Harrison, and John Lennon.

TUNING UP

Hamburg didn't turn out to be quite as glamorous as the Beatles had hoped. The band worked long hours. The club was dingy, and the owner paid them less than promised. But the grueling gig toughened the Beatles and helped improve their stage show. John would later say, "I was raised in Liverpool, but I grew up in Hamburg."

The name *Beatles* was a nod to rock-and-roll legend Buddy Holly's band, the Crickets. One of the band members—some people say John, but not all sources agree—had the idea to change the spelling from "Beetles" to "Beatles." The spelling was a pun on the beat style of pop music popular in 1960s England.

The band returned to Liverpool in December 1960. In March 1961, they landed a job playing at a dank, dark jazz club called the Cavern. Over the next couple of years, the Beatles would play more than two hundred shows there. They gained a growing and devoted following in Liverpool.

On November 9, 1961, Brian Epstein, a Liverpool record shop owner, came to the Cavern to see one of the Beatles' regular lunchtime shows. "I was immediately struck by their music, their beat, and their sense of humor on stage," Epstein later remembered. "Afterwards, when I met them, I was struck again by their personal charm. And it was there that, really, it all started."

Epstein became the band's manager. In May 1962, while the band was playing in Hamburg again, Epstein had good news to report. He sent a telegram saying, "E.M.I. [a record company] contract signed, sealed. Tremendous importance to us all. Wonderful." The Beatles sent Epstein their reactions to the good news on postcards.

Brian Epstein became the manager of the Beatles in 1962. He helped the band bring their music to a wider audience.

McCartney joked, "Please wire . . . advance royalties." George wrote, "Please order four new guitars." And John asked, "When are we going to be millionaires?"

In August 1962, after returning from Hamburg, the Beatles changed their lineup. The band was going to be working with record producer George Martin, who suggested using a more experienced drummer than Pete Best on the recorded tracks. Rather than have one drummer on the records and another at live shows, Epstein and the band opted to replace Best with another talented Liverpool lad. His birth name was Richard Starkey, but he called himself Ringo Starr.

Just as the Beatles were taking off, John's personal life took another dramatic turn. His girlfriend, Cynthia Powell, was pregnant. John and Cynthia were married in a simple civil ceremony on August 23, 1962. McCartney was one of the witnesses who signed the marriage certificate.

The very evening of the wedding, John and the Beatles had a show in Chester, a town south of Liverpool. The newlyweds' wedding night apart would become a pattern in their life together. John was also away on tour on April 8, 1963, when Cynthia gave birth to John Charles Julian Lennon. They called him Julian, a name chosen to honor John's mother.

John poses with his first wife, Cynthia, and their son, Julian, in the late 1960s.

The Beatles, with drummer Ringo Starr, play the Cavern in Liverpool in 1963.

BEATLEMANIA!

The Beatles' fame was skyrocketing. Their first single, "Love Me Do," reached No. 17 on the British charts and the follow-up single, "Please Please Me," rose to the top. Meanwhile, the band traveled around Great Britain playing live shows. In November 1963, they appeared at the Royal Variety Performance. The audience at this prestigious event included the queen and many other members of Great Britain's upper class. John introduced the band's final song with a joke. "The people in the cheaper seats, just clap your hands," he requested. "And the rest of you can just rattle your jewelry."

The demand for the Beatles kept growing. The band was often on television shows and radio, playing their music as well as giving interviews. Their pictures appeared in dozens of magazines and newspapers.

The Beatles rock the *Ed Sullivan Show* on February 9, 1964. This television appearance marked the beginning of Beatlemania in the United States.

Next, the Beatles headed to the United States. On February 9, 1964, they made their first American television appearance, on the popular *Ed Sullivan Show*. The broadcast became one of the most highly rated television programs in history, with an estimated 73 million viewers. A few months later, a U.S. tour began. The frenzy surrounding each public appearance in the United States was unprecedented. Police struggled to hold back the screaming fans. John described it as "like being in the eye of a hurricane."

The band also expanded their horizons into film. They made their first movie, *A Hard Day's Night*, in 1964. The film *Help!* followed the next year. Both movies were full of energy, silly adventure, and lots of music. The movies were popular with fans, although some film critics were less enthusiastic. A reviewer in *Time* magazine described *Help!* as "the Beatles' all-out try at carving a new career as a screen team before their long love affair with the squealers [young, screaming fans] dies out. As such, it is a failure, for as actors they are still nothing but Beatles."

The Beatles also continued to tour, doing shows in Europe and as far away as Australia. In the summer of 1965, a second U.S. tour took place. It was even bigger than the first. The tour's high point was a concert at New York City's Shea Stadium on August 15. More than fifty-five thousand people attended the show, which became legendary for its excitement—and for the deafening screaming of the fans.

Many consider the Beatles' August 15, 1965, show at Shea Stadium in New York to be one of the most legendary concerts in history.

WRITE ON

ohn wrote more than songs. In 1964 he published a book titled *In His Own Write.* The book was a collection of humorous, sometimes nonsensical short stories and essays. A similar volume by John, titled *A Spaniard in the Works,* came out in 1965. Both books included John's drawings alongside his writings.

STIRRING UP CONTROVERSY

The band's fame continued to bring heavy media attention. The group gave hundreds of interviews. John had a reputation for being witty and controversial. In March 1966, for example, he gave an interview to the *London Evening Standard* newspaper. In it, he said, "Christianity will go. It will vanish and shrink. I needn't argue about it; I'm right and I will be proved right. We're more popular than Jesus now; I don't know which will go first—rock 'n' roll or Christianity. Jesus was all right but his disciples [followers] were thick [not smart] and ordinary. It's them [those who follow Christianity] twisting it that ruins it for me."

John's remarks gained little attention in England. But several months later, an American magazine printed the interview. John's comments sparked anger, especially among conservative Christians in the southern United States. Church leaders called for their congregations to burn Beatles records and posters. Some radio stations banned the Beatles' music. The Beatles received threats, and the entire upcoming U.S. tour was at risk. Eventually, Epstein convinced the stubborn John to travel to the United States and apologize for his comments at a press conference.

The tour took place, but the band was fearful of violence. John and Harrison had already grown weary of the craziness that surrounded their shows. The fans couldn't even hear the songs over their own screaming, and the band could barely see the faces of the people they were playing for. The Beatles had thrived on the intimate energy of the gigs at smaller clubs in Liverpool and Hamburg. But as the audiences grew ever larger and more out of control, the magic of playing live faded away, and the band decided not to do so anymore.

Although 1966 marked the end of an era of live Beatles' shows, the band's stardom was far from over. The Beatles continued to produce new albums. One was 1967's *Sgt. Pepper's Lonely Hearts Club Band*. It was more experimental than the band's previous records, using a wide variety of instruments and a range of new recording techniques and effects. Many reviewers raved. *Village Voice* writer Tom Philips praised *Sgt. Pepper's* as "the most ambitious and most successful record album ever issued." Others viewed the album much less favorably. Critic Richard Goldstein, writing in the *New York Times*, described it as "an undistinguished collection of work."

FAREWELL

he Beatles' final live concert took place in San Francisco, California, on August 29, 1966. A crowd of about twenty-four thousand attended the show.

YOKO

On November 9, 1966, John met Japanese American artist Yoko Ono. Her work was on display at a gallery in London. Her pieces were conceptual, abstract, and experimental. For example, one was a ladder leading up to the ceiling. Painted on the ceiling—in such small letters that gallery visitors needed a magnifying glass to see it clearly—was the word "YES." In her art, Yoko often pushed boundaries and provoked strong reactions. As she put it, "I wanted to inspire people and stir people." Yoko was passionate and outspoken about many causes, including world peace, feminism, and equal rights for all people.

John found Yoko fascinating. He later described their meeting. "Imagine two cars . . . heading toward each other and they're gonna crash, head-on. Well, it's like one of those scenes from a film—they're doing a hundred miles an hour [161 kilometers], they both slam their brakes . . . and they stop just in the nick of time, with their bumpers almost touching but not quite. That's what it was like from the first time I got to know her."

When they met, both John and Yoko were married to other people. They stayed in touch and seemed to have a connection. John insisted to his wife that nothing was going on between him and Yoko.

In August 1967, Brian Epstein, the Beatles' manager, died from an accidental drug overdose. Years later, John would say that Epstein's death was a major turning point for the band. "The Beatles were finished when Eppy died. I knew, deep inside me, that was it."

For the time being, though, the band was still going. In 1968 they began work on a record that came to be known as the *White Album*. Meanwhile, John's marriage was crumbling. John admitted to Cynthia that he'd had many affairs with other women during their marriage. In addition, his relationship with Yoko was developing into a romance.

Cynthia also worried about John's drug use and its effect on their family. John often took lysergic acid diethylamide (LSD). The drug produced powerful hallucinations (perceived sounds, sights, or physical sensations). He also smoked marijuana.

After many months of strain, the couple separated. John moved in with Yoko. The Lennons' divorce became official in November. Yoko was divorced from her husband a few months later.

John began bringing Yoko to Beatles' recording sessions. None of the band members had ever brought their girlfriends or wives to these sessions, and Yoko's presence created tension within the group. They saw her presence as an intrusion. John was also devoting more and more time to artistic projects with Yoko. In 1968 the couple put out an experimental album—*Unfinished Music No. 1: Two Virgins*—which they had recorded in a single night. The record used a variety of sound effects and distortion, as well as unscripted speaking and singing by John and Yoko. It gained a lot of attention—not so much for its musical content as for its cover, which showed John and Yoko naked. The next year, in 1969, John and Yoko formed the Plastic Ono Band. The band's membership often changed. Musicians involved at one time or another included Eric Clapton, Keith Moon of the Who, and record producer Phil Spector.

TAKING MUSIC TO BED

On March 20, 1969, John and Yoko married in Gibraltar, a tiny British territory bordering Spain. Knowing they were too famous to have a truly private honeymoon, the couple decided to use their fame to send a political message. Beginning on March 25, the newlyweds held an event they called a "bed-in" at the Hilton hotel in Amsterdam, the Netherlands. Inviting the media into their bedroom, they explained that they intended to spend their whole honeymoon in bed to promote world peace. The couple staged the event, in part, to protest the Vietnam War (1957–1975). The United States became increasingly involved in this controversial Southeast Asian conflict in the early 1960s.

Many observers mocked the bed-in as naive or just plain silly. Nevertheless, in June 1969, John and Yoko held a second bed-in in Montreal, Canada. Once again, the press covered the event, broadcasting reports in Canada and beyond.

During the Montreal bed-in, John wrote a song called "Give Peace a Chance." He recorded it in the hotel

John married Yoko on March 20, 1969. Following their wedding, they spent a week in bed to promote world peace.

room with an audience, many of whom sang and clapped along. The lyrics were simple and the message was direct: "All we are saying is give peace a chance."

IMAGINING A NEW FUTURE

As John explored new artistic and political territory with Yoko, his relationship with the Beatles grew more troubled. Finally, the tension and disharmony reached a breaking point. In September 1969, John told the rest of the Beatles that he was leaving the band. McCartney publicly followed suit a few months later. By the end of 1970, the Beatles no longer existed.

Millions of fans around the world were heartbroken. Many were also angry. Some blamed Yoko, claiming that she'd come between John and the other Beatles. Even well after the band's split, the public's opinion of Yoko remained negative. This bothered John. Elliot Mintz, a disc jockey and reporter, became a close friend of the couple in the early 1970s. Mintz later recalled that John believed the hostility toward Yoko was largely because she was Japanese.

Mintz says that John told him, "If she had blond hair instead of black hair, blue eyes instead of dark eyes . . . if she wasn't a feminist and [Japanese], then they'd say she was beautiful."

In 1971 John released the album *Imagine*. That same year, John and Yoko moved to New York City. They intended the move to be temporary, while Yoko tried to regain custody of Kyoko, her daughter from her previous marriage. Yoko's ex-husband had disappeared with the girl, despite that the court had awarded Yoko full custody. (John's child, Julian, was in Cynthia Lennon's custody.) But the couple felt more and more at home in New York. Yoko already knew the city well. She had gone to college nearby and had later worked in the city. She shared her knowledge with John. "She made me walk around the streets and parks and squares and examine every nook and cranny," John said. "You could say I fell in love with New York on a street corner."

Not everyone was happy about the star calling the United States home. The former Beatle was a hugely influential voice around the globe, and his political activities against the Vietnam War bothered some Americans.

In March 1972, John learned that he was to be deported from (forced to leave) the United States. Lawyers representing the U.S. government claimed that a past drug conviction was the reason for his deportation. But John felt—and many observers agreed—that he was being targeted because of his political views. John and Yoko spoke out loudly about the need for peace and for the United States to get out of the Vietnam War. In addition, they had become friends with a number of more radical antiwar activists.

John hired immigration lawyer Leon Wildes to represent him in the deportation case. Wildes warned John that winning would not be easy. But Wildes

John flashes the peace sign as he walks into the U.S. Immigration and Naturalization Service office in New York City in May 1972 to fight his deportation case.

worked hard for his famous client. After years of fighting the deportation, John and Wildes finally won their case in 1975. A written statement by Judge Irving R. Kaufman said, "If in our two hundred years of independence we have in some measure realized our ideals, it is in large part because we have always found a place for those committed to the spirit of liberty, and willing to help implement it. John's four-year battle to remain in our country is testimony to his faith in the American dream."

On October 9, 1975, a few hours after learning that John would be able to stay in the United States permanently, Yoko gave birth to a boy. The couple named their son—who shared his father's birthday—Sean Taro Ono Lennon. John was ecstatic. "I feel higher than the Empire State Building," he gushed.

THE LAST VERSE

After Sean's birth, Yoko reportedly told her husband that she had done her part. At the age of forty-two and after several miscarriages, she had carried Sean through nine months of pregnancy. Now it was John's turn to care for the boy. Yoko had a good head for business and finance, so she took charge of the couple's many business affairs. Meanwhile, John— who was eager for some time out of the spotlight—devoted himself to raising his second son. He became a househusband, taking the baby for walks in Central Park and learning to bake bread.

John enjoyed his closeness with Sean. He was able to create a father-son relationship that he had never had with his own father or with Julian. But by the time Sean was about five years old, John was eager to get back to music. On a trip to Bermuda in the summer of 1980, he returned to songwriting. He would telephone Yoko to sing and play his new songs for her. Yoko, too, began writing pieces of her own. When John got back to New York, the couple began recording their new songs.

The result was John's first album in more than five years. Titled *Double Fantasy*, it came out in November 1980.

A WORD OF **ADVICE**

ou make your own dream. That's the Beatles story, isn't it? That's the Yoko Story. That's what I'm saying now. Produce your own dream. If you want to save Peru, go save Peru. It's quite possible to do anything, but not if you put it on the leaders and the parking meters. Don't expect [Presidents] Carter or Reagan or John Lennon or Yoko Ono or Bob Dylan or Jesus Christ to come and do it for you. You have to do it yourself."

—John Lennon, September 1980

It featured fourteen tracks—seven by John and seven by Yoko. John was thrilled with the album, but he was not done. On the evening of December 8, 1980, John and Yoko were back at work in the studio.

A few hours later, John Lennon was dead.

John Lennon and Yoko Ono released *Double Fantasy* in November 1980. It would be the last album John made.

CHAPTER **TWO**

"GIVE **PEACE** a **CHANCE**"

> Your way of life is a political statement.
>
> —JOHN LENNON, N.D.

John Lennon grew up during a period of great change and upheaval. World War II for example, had brought horror and devastation to communities around the world. Although no one knows exactly how many people died, estimates begin at about 50 million and range to more than 70 million. In addition to the unheard of loss of life, the war had left some parts of Europe and Asia in ruins. Families were uprooted, if not destroyed, leading to massive human relocation around the globe.

COLD SNAP

Even as the world recovered from one war, a new conflict—known as the Cold War (1945–1991)—began. This was a period of intense competition and suspicion between Communist and non-Communist nations. Communism is a political, social, and economic model based on the idea that property should be state-owned rather than private. The Communist model also says that all citizens should have equal resources and be of equal social status. (Capitalism, in contrast, is based on ideas of free trade and individual property.)

Some Communist leaders sought to spread their way of governing. Non-Communist countries worked to discourage this expansion. The conflict was especially fierce between the Communist Soviet Union and the strongly anti-Communist United States. Labeled "cold" because it never erupted into a "hot," or military, war between the two nations, the Cold War nevertheless had a direct—and often damaging—effect on many other countries.

Especially in the United States, the Cold War deeply affected people's mind-sets and moods. Both the United States and the Soviet Union had nuclear weapons. The United States had first used these powerful weapons during World War II. In 1945 U.S. bombers had dropped nuclear bombs on the Japanese cities of Hiroshima and Nagasaki. The bombing attacks killed more than 150,000 people and flattened both cities.

Since the two main players in the Cold War both had nuclear weapons, the military strategy was called mutual assured destruction (MAD). That means that if either country launched a nuclear weapon—for any reason—the other would fire back. The resulting conflict would be so fierce that both nations would probably be destroyed.

John Lennon was just a boy when the Cold War was tightening its grip on American society. Europeans felt the fear too. The British government, like that of the United States, was anti-Communist. As the Cold War continued, some activists in Britain and the United States began to protest nuclear weapons.

WAR AND PEACE

Some Americans sought comfort, stability, and convention in the postwar years. But others were eager for change. A thriving counterculture attracted people who wanted to explore new ideas and lifestyles. New York City was one of the centers of this counterculture. A neighborhood there known as

Greenwich Village has long been a popular spot in New York for artists and activists. This photograph shows a Greenwich Village street corner in 1966.

Greenwich Village was a haven for artists, musicians, writers, and political activists. San Francisco, California, was another hot spot.

The energy and drive for change gained momentum in the 1960s as the Vietnam War escalated. U.S. involvement in this conflict grew out of Cold War competition. North Vietnam was Communist and was fighting to take control of non-Communist South Vietnam to create a single Communist state. Worried about the spread of Communism, the United States backed the South Vietnamese resistance. Meanwhile, the Soviet Union aided the North.

The Vietnam conflict was the first American war to be covered heavily on television news. Graphic images of violence, death, and suffering were broadcast

Three wounded U.S. soldiers wait for a medical evacuation helicopter in Vietnam in 1968. Televised images of the ravages of war alarmed and motivated many Americans, who protested the United States' involvement in the war in this faraway country.

to American homes each night. Horrified and saddened by what they saw, many students and activists protested U.S. involvement in the war. Opposition to the war was not confined to the United States. Protests took place in Britain and other European nations as well.

FALLEN HEROES

On November 22, 1963, U.S. president John F. Kennedy was assassinated in Dallas, Texas. Kennedy (often called JFK) had embodied an optimistic and idealistic outlook. He was the second-youngest president in U.S. history, and he supported the civil rights movement. His sudden death shook the entire nation.

In 1968 the country lost two more civil rights leaders. Martin Luther King Jr. was assassinated in Memphis, Tennessee, on April 4. Just two months later, Senator

Robert F. Kennedy was also assassinated. Robert Kennedy was JFK's younger brother and was a candidate for president.

The deaths of these three leaders left many Americans angry, frightened, and disillusioned. Yet the movement for social change and for world peace didn't end. In August 1968, the Democratic National Convention was held in Chicago, Illinois. Massive protests for peace and social justice gripped the city. The protests began peacefully but turned ugly when violence erupted between police and protesters. In the rioting that followed, police beat some of the protesters. Like the images of the war, television and newspaper images of the violence at the convention angered Americans.

Meanwhile, the Vietnam War dragged on. Thousands of U.S. soldiers died. Thousands more were drafted to fight. The threat of nuclear war hovered over the nation. On February 27, 1968, news broadcaster Walter Cronkite commented on the situation. Cronkite said, "It seems now more certain than ever that the bloody experience of Vietnam is to end in a stalemate. This summer's almost certain standoff will either end in real give-and-take negotiation or terrible escalation. And for every means we have to escalate, the enemy can match us. . . . And with each escalation, the world comes closer to the brink of cosmic disaster."

FROM ROCKER TO REVOLUTIONARY

Living in these turbulent times, John became a prominent peace activist. He grew more and more committed to using his fame to send a message. As John told reporter Gloria Emerson of the *New York Times* in 1969, "If I'm gonna get on the front page, I might as well get on the front page with the word 'peace.'"

FLOWER POWER

Counterculture poet Allen Ginsberg coined the term *flower power* in the 1960s. It referred to using peaceful protest to bring about change. The idea of flower power spread quickly. Antiwar activists carried flowers, wore them on their clothes and in their hair, and even had the slogan printed on T-shirts.

John was very successful in doing just that. His 1969 song "Give Peace a Chance" became an anthem for the antiwar movement. For example, the Moratorium to End the War in Vietnam took place on October 15, 1969. In cities all across the United States, tens of thousands of people joined marches and rallies for peace. One month later, another huge antiwar demonstration took place in Washington, D.C. An estimated three hundred thousand or more people took part, making the event the largest political gathering in U.S. history. Popular folk musician Pete Seeger led the massive crowd in singing "Give Peace a Chance."

Peace demonstrations intensified in April 1970, when President Richard Nixon gave orders to invade Cambodia as part of the Vietnam

Demonstrators gather outside the Colorado State Capitol in Denver on October 15, 1969, to join in the Moratorium to End the War in Vietnam.

War. Shortly thereafter, on May 1, 1970, students at Kent State University in Ohio began protesting the Cambodian invasion. That night, after looting and vandalism began on campus, city officials called in the Ohio National Guard. Tensions rose for several days, peaking on May 4 when members of the National Guard fired at a crowd of students and other protesters on the university campus. The soldiers killed four student protesters and wounded nine others.

Events like these only caused John and Yoko to become more involved in the peace movement. They began spending time with prominent antiwar activists Jerry

Rubin and Abbie Hoffman. In December 1971, along with Rubin, John and Yoko took part in a rally in Ann Arbor, Michigan. The rally's goal was to free civil rights activist John Sinclair. In 1969 Sinclair had been sentenced to ten years in prison for giving marijuana to an undercover police officer. Many observers believed that his sentence was too harsh. They thought that the police and the courts had targeted him because of his activism.

Before performing a song he'd written for the occasion, John spoke to the crowd. He said, "We came here, not only to help John and to spotlight what's going on, but also to show and to say to all of you that apathy isn't it, and that we can do something. Okay, so 'Flower Power' didn't work—so what. We start again."

The event had a quick and dramatic effect. As Sinclair himself later recalled, "Everything just skyrocketed . . . the tide of public opinion turned in my favor." Three days later, Sinclair was released from prison. Many felt that John's presence had been a major influence.

FOLLOWING HIS EVERY MOVE

Meanwhile, John began to believe that the U.S. government was monitoring him. He said,

> I'm not saying they had plans other than just keeping tabs on me, to see what I was up to, who I was seeing. But I felt followed everywhere by government agents. Every time I picked up my phone there was a lot of noise. Somebody gave me a number that if you call it, you get this feedback sound that confirms your phone is being tapped. And I did it and it did. Suddenly I realized this was serious, they were coming for me, one way or another. They were harassing me. I'd open the door and there'd be guys standing on the other side of the street. I'd get in the car and they'd be following me and not hiding. That's what got me paranoid. They wanted me to see I was being followed.

John *did* sound a little paranoid. But he was also right. For example, informants for the U.S. Federal Bureau of Investigation (FBI) had been at the Michigan rally for John Sinclair. (The FBI is a U.S. government agency that deals with internal national security.) FBI documents from the period clearly show that the agency was interested in John and his activities. FBI files on John include transcripts of his television appearances, as well as notes about his comings and goings.

Government records also suggest, as many people suspected, that John's deportation case was indeed tied to his politics. U.S. officials viewed some of John's friendships with deep suspicion. An Immigration and Naturalization Service (INS) document from this period reported on John's and Yoko's "relations with one . . . Jerry Rubin, and one John Sinclair . . . also their many commitments which are judged to be political and unfavorable to the present administration. . . . Because of this and their controversial behavior [Lennon and Ono] are to be judged as both undesirable and dangerous aliens."

Lawyer Leon Wildes recounts, "We ultimately were able to examine the records in the case, and, lo and behold, deep in John's immigration file, which was a high-security file, were documents reaching all the way up to President Nixon, showing improper interference in an immigration case and prejudgment."

John's worries about being followed did not stop him from speaking his mind. Near the end of 1971, John, Yoko, and the Plastic Ono Band released a song titled "Happy Xmas (War Is Over)." John and Yoko also published posters and rented billboards that read,

WAR IS OVER! IF YOU WANT IT
Happy Christmas from John & Yoko

The message appeared on billboards in eleven major cities around the world.

Meanwhile, John continued to participate in marches and other demonstrations for peace. In addition to demanding an end to the Vietnam War, activists also called for the United States to get rid of or reduce the number of its nuclear weapons.

John and Yoko rented billboards to spread their message of peace in December 1971. This billboard appeared in New York City.

Some people believed that Yoko was the force behind John's political activity. But John challenged this assumption. He said, "I've always been politically minded and against the status quo. It's pretty basic when you're brought up like I was, to hate and fear the police as a natural enemy and despise the army as something that takes everybody away and leaves them dead somewhere. I mean, it's just a basic working-class thing. . . . In my case I've never *not* been political."

William Ernest Pobjoy, one of John's headmasters (principals) at Quarry Bank High School, believes that John's politics had roots in his youth. As Pobjoy put it, "I think [John] always had sympathy for the underdog, because I think he saw himself—virtually an orphan—as being an underdog."

"THE WHOLE WORLD'S CHANGED"

In 1972 President Nixon—a Republican—was running for reelection. His handling of the Vietnam War had become very unpopular— especially among young Americans. With the passage of the Twenty-sixth Amendment to the U.S. Constitution the year before, young Americans gained political power. The amendment lowered the voting age in presidential elections from twenty-one to eighteen. Suddenly, the United States had more than ten million new voters. Many of those voters were the same people who listened to John Lennon's music—and were influenced by his politics.

MUSIC WITH A **MESSAGE**

ohn knew that his politics weren't popular with everyone. But he also understood that his music was a powerful tool. He pointed to his song "Imagine" as an example of this power. As John put it, "'Imagine' is a big hit almost everywhere—anti-religious, anti-nationalistic, anti-conventional, anti-capitalistic, but because it is sugar-coated, it is accepted. Now I understand what you have to do: put your political message across with a little honey."

The new amendment threatened Nixon's chances of winning the race since many of the new young voters were Democrats. Nixon's team also worried about another threat. The Republican National Convention was scheduled for August 1972. Political activists were planning protests, as well as a nationwide concert tour leading up to the convention. Many expected John to play on the tour. Although he denied that he would be involved—partly because of his ongoing deportation case—rumors continued to swirl.

In the end, demonstrations took place, but the concert tour did not. Nixon won the 1972 election by a landslide. But scandal marked his second term. In June—a few months before the election—police arrested five men. The men had broken into Democratic National Committee headquarters at the Watergate office building complex in Washington, DC. Nixon's reelection team was connected to the break-in, but they—and Nixon himself—denied knowledge of the break-in. But televised hearings in the summer of 1973 revealed that the president and his staff had, in fact, directed the break-in and broken laws in an attempt to cover their tracks. In August 1974, Nixon left office in disgrace, announcing his resignation on live television. His vice president, Gerald Ford, became president and finished the term.

The Vietnam War finally ended in April 1975. Many people believed that the protests and peace demonstrations had helped lead the United States to withdraw from the conflict. But the war had scarred the nation. The brutal conflict had cost thousands of lives and millions of dollars. U.S. soldiers—many of them badly wounded both physically and emotionally—came home to face anger and scorn at their involvement in an unpopular war.

Democrat Jimmy Carter won the 1976 presidential election. His politics were very different from Nixon's.

After the scandal and war of the Nixon years, voters hoped that Carter would represent a new beginning. But ultimately, people saw Carter as ineffective. As the 1980s began, the presidency changed hands again. Republican Ronald Reagan won the 1980 presidential election. An actor turned politician, Ronald Reagan was the former governor of California.

John later spoke about the turmoil of those decades. He mused, "The thing the sixties did was show us the possibility and the responsibility that we all had. It wasn't the answer, it just gave us a glimpse of the possibility." He added, "You have to give thanks to God or whatever is up there to the fact that we all survived. We all survived Vietnam or Watergate, the tremendous upheaval of the whole world . . . the world is not like the sixties, the whole world's changed. I am going into an unknown future, but I'm still all here. And still, while there's life, there's hope."

CHAPTER THREE

STORY OF an ASSASSIN

> Somehow he seemed so innocent looking.

—WALTER NEWTON HENDRIX,
A CHILDHOOD FRIEND OF
MARK DAVID CHAPMAN, 1988

Mark David Chapman grew up in a distant nation and a different era from the man he would eventually assassinate. Fifteen years younger than John Lennon, he was born on May 10, 1955, in Fort Worth, Texas. Mark's father, David, was stationed in Texas as a staff sergeant in the U.S. Air Force. Diane Chapman, Mark's mother, was a nurse. Soon after Mark was born, his father left the military and the family moved to Indiana, where Mark's father pursued a college degree in engineering.

"NORMAL"

After Mark's father earned his degree, he found a job in Georgia. The Chapmans moved to Decatur, a suburb of Atlanta. When Mark was seven years old, Diane and David had a second child, Susan.

Mark David Chapman, shown here at the age of twenty, grew up with his parents and younger sister in Decatur, Georgia.

From the outside, Mark seemed to have a normal childhood. But some of his memories paint a different picture. He later recalled, "I don't think I ever hugged my father. He never told me he loved me, and he never said he was sorry." Chapman went on, "He never showed any emotional love. . . . Mom always told me that my father couldn't show these kinds of things but he'd try in other ways. You know, he was always home and he never drank and things like that, but I needed more than just a father who was responsible."

Mark also said that his father had been physically abusive toward him and especially toward Mark's mother. Mark recalled nights when his mother would cry out to her son for help.

Diane Chapman didn't entirely share her son's view of their family life. She later confirmed that her husband had sometimes abused her. But she also stated flatly, "I pretty well know there was nothing that drastic in our lives that would cause anything like [our son killing John Lennon]. As far as I can see, we were pretty normal. It's true that Dave didn't show his emotions, but he would do anything for Mark. That's where it's so unfair. What more did you want from a person? Did you want total understanding? Who gets that? My father didn't even look up from the paper at me half the time. I didn't care."

Mark and Diane also offered different accounts of his social isolation. Mark said that he had trouble at school—where he was bullied—as well as at home. Yet his mother's memories were different. She felt her son was not isolated. "I've seen him described as being a loner," she said. "Are you kidding? He had lots of friends. I never had to tell him to go out and play. And when he was inside he was always on the couch talking to me. I was the one who wanted to be the loner." Diane also described her son as an active child who enjoyed playing guitar and collecting coins.

Diane was not alone in thinking that all was well with her son. Walter Newton Hendrix knew Mark from school in Decatur. "There was nothing about Mark's behavior, nothing he ever said to me, that would make me want to say: 'John Lennon had better be careful because he's coming after him.' Nothing he ever did that made me think he would not end up just a normal person."

Yet as Mark himself pointed out, "Normal kids don't grow up to shoot ex-Beatles."

THE LITTLE PEOPLE

As a teenager, Mark—like so many other kids his age in the 1960s—enjoyed the music of the Beatles. He played the band's albums and put up Beatles posters in his room. His father had taught him to play the guitar, and Mark liked to perform Beatles tunes.

But Mark also had a dark side. As an adult, Mark would speak frequently of death and anger when describing his childhood. Somber images seemed to dominate his memories. For example, he recalled, "I found this turtle shell half-buried in the ground. It was empty. I remember picking it up and cleaning out the dirt and looking at it for a long, long time. What had happened to the life that had been there? This had to be death. But what did that mean?"

When Mark felt gloomy, lonely, or powerless, he found some comfort in an imaginary world. For as long as he could remember, he had imagined beings he called the Little People. They lived inside the walls of his home, with jobs and shops and schools of their own.

"The Little People adored me," Mark told writer Jack Jones. "I got my respect and adulation from an imaginary source, rather than confronting the kids and the things that hurt me."

Mark added, "When I got really angry about something, I would take it out on the Little People. . . . I had a button on the arm of the couch in the den. When I pushed it, it would blow up the houses where the Little People lived. Sometimes I would kill hundreds or thousands of them. Then, after I calmed down later, I would apologize. They would always forgive me."

A PERSONALITY SPLIT

By the time Mark reached his early teens, he lacked direction. He began experimenting with drugs in about 1969. At Columbia High School, he made friends with other kids who were into drugs. "For the first time in my life . . . I was part of a group," he later said. Mark started smoking marijuana and taking LSD regularly. His attitude quickly changed. "All of a sudden he was anti-parent, anti-everything,"

remembered his mother. "He stopped going to school, and I just let him go. There didn't seem anything we could do to stop him."

Mark's behavior worried his parents. They were even more worried when he ran away from home at the age of fourteen. He went to Miami, Florida, where he stayed for about two weeks.

Within a couple of years, however, Mark changed his focus completely. When he was about sixteen years old, he turned to religion. He became a born-again Christian, attending prayer meetings and religious retreats. The change was so drastic that one friend described it as "a true personality split."

Mark seemed to have found purpose and peace in his new faith. It did, however, diminish his love of the Beatles. He took offense at John's remark about Jesus and Christianity being less popular than the Beatles. He also disliked the song "Imagine." He still loved music, but he shifted his adoration to the rock musician Todd Rundgren. Rundgren released many successful albums in the 1970s. His early style had a pop sound, and he later developed a heavier, more rock-oriented sound and explored jazz.

Chapman also discovered another book that influenced him deeply besides the Bible. Around 1971 he read the J. D. Salinger novel *The Catcher in the Rye*. Originally published in 1951, the book is a popular, controversial work about a sensitive, angry, and confused teenager named Holden Caulfield. Chapman immediately felt a connection to Holden and to the book. He later said, "I was very highly moved by it. I guess I was kind of like Holden in those days too, and I kind of was afraid of growing up. I wanted to shut my eyes to the bad and evil of the world."

Mark also got involved with the Young Men's Christian Association (YMCA—often called simply the Y). In 1972 he worked as a counselor at a summer camp of the South DeKalb YMCA in Decatur. He was good at the job, and the experience gave him new confidence.

One former camper remembered Mark with great fondness. "The other kids were so outgoing and everything, they kind of scared me to death," she said. "[Mark] saw that and took me under his wing. He'd take me aside and we'd go shoot arrows and things. I remember I really hated swimming, but he taught me to swim.... He was about the best friend I had when I was growing up, and he was the nicest person I think I've ever known. I could see no wrong in that guy at all."

THE CATCHER
IN THE RYE

J. D. SALINGER

The Catcher in the Rye was originally published in 1951. Since its publication, it has frequently been banned in schools and libraries for obscene language and for sexual content.

J. D. SALINGER

J. D. Salinger was born as Jerome David Salinger in New York City in 1919. As a boy, Salinger revealed a talent for writing. He wrote for his high school newspaper and also began writing short stories. After high school, Salinger briefly attended two different colleges and held a variety of jobs. In 1942 he joined the U.S. Army and fought in World War II.

Throughout these years, Salinger had continued to write. He'd submitted many of his stories to the *New Yorker* magazine—and he'd gotten a lot of rejection slips in return. But eventually he succeeded in getting some of his stories published in the prestigious magazine. Then, in 1951, he published *The Catcher in the Rye.* Teenager Holden Caulfield narrates the book, describing his struggle to determine who he is and where he fits in the world.

Critics had mixed opinions of the novel. Reviewer Nash K. Burger wrote in the *New York Times,* "Holden's story is told in Holden's own strange, wonderful language by J.D. Salinger in an unusually brilliant novel." But another critic, James Stern, mimicked Salinger's style in a negative review for the same newspaper. Stern wrote, "This book though, it's too long. Gets kind of monotonous."

Salinger next published *Nine Stories,* a collection of short stories, in 1953. That same year, he moved from New York City to the small town of Cornish, New Hampshire. Two years later, he married Claire Douglas. The couple had two children before divorcing in 1967. Meanwhile, Salinger wrote two more books. *Franny and Zooey* came out in 1961, and *Raise High the Roof Beam, Carpenters and Seymour: An Introduction* was published in 1963. These would be the last books that Salinger published. Though he continued to write, he refused to publish another book. He became more and more protective of his privacy and granted very few interviews during the following decades. Salinger died in Cornish in 2010.

In addition to being a camp counselor, Mark did other work for the Y. He taught guitar lessons and helped raise funds for the organization. One of the people Mark worked with was Tony Adams, the director of the South DeKalb Y. He saw great potential in Mark. And he shared the general view of Mark and the Chapmans. "I'd say it was a very happy family and Mark was a happy, well-adjusted boy."

THE PIED PIPER

Chapman graduated from Columbia High School in 1973. He enrolled at a community college in Decatur but dropped out after a short time.

His job at the YMCA, however, was still going very well. He continued to earn praise for his work with children. "Mark was a pied piper [someone people would follow] with the kids," Adams said. "I've never seen anybody who was as conscientious about his job and as close to children as he was."

In the summer of 1975, Chapman's work took him on an international journey. He and a few other YMCA counselors spent the summer at a Y branch in Beirut, Lebanon. For Chapman, it was the trip of a lifetime. But the trip turned out to be short. A civil war had begun in Lebanon that spring. When it intensified, the Y evacuated the young counselors. The trip was frightening, but it also gave Chapman a taste of dangerous adventure. Back in Decatur, he listened to the sound of gunfire in Beirut, which he had taped while there.

That same summer, Chapman found love. He started dating Jessica Blankenship, a girl he had known since grade school. Like Mark, Jessica was a devout Christian. Their relationship soon grew serious.

In August 1975, Chapman began working at a YMCA-run camp in Fort Chaffee, Arkansas. This camp's purpose was to resettle Vietnamese refugees who had fled from the Vietnam War. Chapman was very popular with the children at Fort Chaffee. His dedication impressed those around him. One coworker said that Chapman was "probably the most diligent worker with the refugees [at Fort Chaffee]." The YMCA director of the camp, David

Moore, became a friend and mentor to Chapman. Moore described the twenty-year-old Chapman as "one of the most compassionate, sensitive young people I've ever met."

Chapman and Jessica wrote to each other during the months that Chapman was at Fort Chaffee. She also visited him once in the fall. But around then, Jessica later said, she "started noticing that [Mark] was just having a lot of struggles with himself. It was like a big war was going on inside him."

That war took a toll. Just as things had been going well for Chapman, they all started to fall apart. In 1976 the twenty-one-year-old Chapman enrolled at Covenant College, a small Christian school in Lookout Mountain, Georgia. Jessica was already a student there. But Chapman struggled at Covenant just as he had at community college. He grew depressed. Even working at the Y no longer appealed to him.

Chapman decided to try something new. He found work as a security guard. At his first job, he was an unarmed guard. He went on to take training and pass the tests necessary to carry a gun. Jessica didn't like this new Mark, and the couple soon broke up.

TICKET TO PARADISE

Chapman continued to battle depression. He decided that he no longer wanted to live. In 1977 he traveled to Hawaii, where he planned to kill himself. When he got there, however, he started to

Chapman gives a child a ride on his shoulders at a YMCA camp in Fort Chaffee, Arkansas, in 1975. Chapman was popular with children and coworkers at the camp.

feel better. He stayed in a nice hotel near the beach and soaked up Hawaii's beauty. After a week or so, he went home to Georgia. He didn't stay there for long. Chapman soon returned to Hawaii. He wanted to get a job and make a home there.

Chapman's depression reappeared, however. He attempted, unsuccessfully, to take his own life. It was clear he wasn't well. On June 21, 1977, he checked into Castle Memorial Hospital (later renamed Castle Medical Center) in Kailua, Hawaii. With the help of medical professionals, his condition improved.

Chapman's time at Castle Memorial did more than mend his mental health. It also led to a job. Chapman had made friends during his stay. After first becoming a volunteer at the hospital, he began working in the maintenance department. One of his bosses at Castle Memorial later said, "Mark was a good worker who was well-liked." Another recalled, "All the patients, particularly the older ones that nobody else would talk to, just loved that boy."

Early in 1978, Chapman was earning money and feeling good. That summer he set off on a trip around the world. Stops on his six-week itinerary included Japan, Thailand, India, Israel, Switzerland, France, and England.

TO WHOM IT MAY **CONCERN**

Even people who were close to Chapman saw no signs that he might be dangerous or unstable. For example, on Chapman's 1978 trip around the world, he carried a letter from David Moore introducing him and recommending him to YMCA staff at some international Y facilities where Chapman planned to stay. The letter read,

This is to introduce Mark Chapman, a staff member of the US International Division of the National Council of YMCAs. Mark was an effective and dedicated worker at the refugee camp in Fort Chaffee Arkansas. . . . I can commend him to you as a sincere and intelligent young man. Any assistance that you can give Mark during his travels will be greatly appreciated.

Gloria Abe married Mark David Chapman in 1979.

While planning this vacation, Chapman had taken a liking to his travel agent, Gloria Abe. She was a Japanese American woman a few years older than Chapman. During the trip, Chapman and Abe exchanged letters. After he returned to Hawaii, they began dating. In early 1979, Chapman asked Abe to marry him. She agreed and the couple was married that June. Meanwhile, Chapman's mother, who had divorced her husband, had joined him in Hawaii. Chapman enjoyed having his mother close.

DARK CLOUDS

Once again, it seemed that things were looking up for Chapman. He had a job and a wife, and he lived in one of the world's most beautiful places. He even got a better-paying job, in Castle Memorial's community relations department.

But once again, the good times didn't last. Chapman began to act strangely. Gloria later said that her husband became abusive. She recalls him making threatening phone calls to strangers in Hawaii. He also forced her to quit her job at the travel agency. She found a job at Castle Memorial, and the couple took the bus together to work each day.

The duties of Chapman's new position at the hospital included working in the print shop, producing documents. The job sparked an interest in art. Chapman began collecting pieces, beginning with fairly modest purchases. But the new hobby soon grew well beyond Chapman's means. He borrowed money to feed his hunger for new pieces, including $7,500 for a Norman Rockwell print.

Chapman's temper grew short, and he was prone to violent outbursts. He started drinking heavily. In late 1979, he quit his job and found work as a security guard at a Honolulu condominium building.

During these troubled days, Chapman spent a lot of time at the library. In the autumn of 1980, he spotted *The Catcher in the Rye* on the shelves. Although the book had meant a great deal to him during his teens, he had not read it for years. He plunged into it again and found it more powerful than ever. His old identification with Holden Caulfield surged back.

Chapman also found another book at the library, *John Lennon: One Day at a Time*. A biography of John Lennon by author Anthony Fawcett, the book included many photographs. A lot of the shots showed John in New York, posing in front of the Statue of Liberty or standing on the roof of the Dakota. According to Chapman, reading that book triggered something in him. He later said that he felt betrayed by John. He felt like Holden Caulfield of *Catcher in the Rye*. Holden sees the adult world as corrupt and full of "phonies." To Chapman, John had apparently become just such a phony. "[John] told us to imagine no possessions," Chapman said, "and there he was, with millions of dollars . . . laughing at people like me who had believed the lies and bought the records.

"At some point, at the looking of those pictures, I became enraged at [John] . . . something inside me just broke."

CHAPTER FOUR

DEATH on THE DOORSTEP

I just pulled the trigger steady five times.

—MARK DAVID CHAPMAN, 1980

n October 1980, a few weeks after Chapman had read the Anthony Fawcett book on Lennon, he began making plans for a trip. An idea had formed in his mind—a way that he could get rid of one of the world's "phonies." He would kill John Lennon.

Chapman told his wife that he was going to New York City—alone. The couple's finances were shaky, so Chapman borrowed money to make the trip. He quit his security guard job, telling his boss that he planned to travel. He ended his last shift at the job on October 23. As usual, he signed out in the company's logbook. But it wasn't quite the usual signature. Rather than writing his own name, he wrote "John Lennon." Then he crossed out the entry and walked out the door.

Chapman had a few errands to take care of before leaving town. On October 27, he went to a gun shop in Honolulu. He bought a .38 caliber revolver for $169. The gun held five shots and had a short, 2-inch (5-centimeter) barrel. It was a small but powerful gun that was easy to hide. Like most revolvers, the .38 was effective only at close range. He then went to a local police department for a gun license, which he got

TOP: This photo shows the "John Lennon" signature that Chapman faked to sign out from work on October 23, 1980.

BOTTOM: Chapman bought this .38 caliber handgun in Honolulu, Hawaii, before heading to New York.

without difficulty. Two days later, he boarded a flight to New York. His ticket was one-way.

TAKE ONE

Chapman arrived in New York City on October 29, 1980. He checked in at the Waldorf Astoria, a fancy hotel in midtown Manhattan. To Chapman, the Waldorf was more than just a grand old hotel. It was also somewhere Holden Caulfield had stayed in *The Catcher in the Rye.*

Chapman had come to New York with a mission, but he also took time to see some sights. He went to several plays and visited the Statue of Liberty, the Empire State Building, and Central Park.

And of course, he went to the Dakota. When he asked the building's doormen if John Lennon was in town, they told him little. They knew that autograph seekers were common in the neighborhood. The posh Dakota building was home to many celebrities other than John, including composer Leonard Bernstein, actress Lauren Bacall, and singer-songwriter Roberta Flack.

Although Chapman had brought his gun to New York, he had not brought bullets. But once he arrived in New York, he learned that only residents of New York could legally purchase ammunition there.

For a moment, Chapman's plans seemed to crumble before his eyes. But then an idea struck him: he could visit an old friend of his who still lived in Georgia. The friend, Dana Reeves, was a sheriff's deputy. Chapman knew that he would have ammunition.

So Chapman traveled to Georgia for the weekend. While he was there, he saw several old acquaintances, including the parents of his former girlfriend Jessica Blankenship. One friend said that Chapman seemed to be in a good mood during their short visit. But others said he seemed depressed.

As expected, Reeves had bullets. Chapman asked him for five hollow-point bullets, known for their especially deadly force. Unlike most bullets, hollow points expand when they enter the body, doing great internal damage. Chapman told Reeves that he wanted them for self-defense in New York City, and the two friends practiced target shooting.

After his Georgia weekend, Chapman flew back to New York. He didn't stay at the expensive Waldorf this time, choosing the cheaper Olcott Hotel. Later, he moved again, to a YMCA. He continued to visit the Dakota to wait for the right moment. One night he went to a

This photograph shows five hollow-point bullets after they have been fired from a gun. They are designed to do maximum damage on impact.

movie theater, where he saw *Ordinary People.* The popular film, which focused on a suicidal teenager and his family, affected Chapman deeply. He remembered his wife and her love for him. He had second thoughts about his plan. Later that night, he called his wife and told her that he was coming home soon. He told her that he had wanted to kill John Lennon, but that Gloria's love had saved him. Confused and frightened, Gloria did not call the police or any other authorities. She simply pleaded with Chapman to come home. Without having spotted John, Chapman returned to Hawaii on November 12.

TAKE TWO

Back in Hawaii, Chapman's violent urges returned. He couldn't shake his obsessive thoughts about killing John Lennon. He bought another airline ticket and told his wife that he was going back to New York to look for a job.

Chapman arrived in New York for the second time on Saturday, December 6, 1980. He checked into the YMCA on West 63rd Street. The Y was cheap—a room cost only about sixteen dollars a night. It was also convenient, just nine blocks from the Dakota.

While in New York this second time, Chapman thought about killing himself in a dramatic fashion. He considered shooting himself at the top of the Statue of Liberty. "No one else had killed themselves there before," he reasoned. "I wanted to go out in a blaze of glory."

But Chapman didn't act on those thoughts. He stayed focused on Lennon. On his first day in town, he went to the Dakota almost right away to take up his watch for Lennon. When he got there, he met a couple of dedicated Lennon fans. Chapman told them that he hoped to get John's autograph. They recommended that Chapman buy a copy of Lennon's *Double Fantasy* album for John to sign. Chapman waited there much of the day but never saw him.

That night Chapman felt uncomfortable at the Y. The next morning—Sunday, December 7—he checked out and moved to a Sheraton. The hotel was much more expensive than the Y, but he felt calmer there.

That day, carrying a copy of *Double Fantasy,* he returned to the Dakota.

But for the second day in a row, he waited for hours with no result. Giving up for the day, he headed back to the Sheraton.

MAKING A STATEMENT

On the morning of Monday, December 8, Chapman prepared to return to his post outside John's apartment. Before leaving his hotel room, he carefully laid out a display of objects on the dresser. One of the items was Chapman's Bible, in which he had made a change. On the first page of "The Gospel According to John," Chapman had added the name "Lennon," so that it read, "The Gospel According to John Lennon." Chapman also left his expired passport, a tape of Todd Rundgren's music, and a letter from Chapman's YMCA supervisor at Fort Chaffee. In addition, he laid out a picture of himself with some of the Vietnamese children he'd worked with at Fort Chaffee. Another photograph showed the 1965 Chevrolet that Chapman had driven during his high school years. And finally, he left a small picture of Dorothy and the Cowardly Lion from the classic 1939 musical film *The Wizard of Oz*.

Chapman was careful about the way he arranged this collection of items. He recalled, "I practiced what it was going to look like when police officers came into the room."

He went on, "I woke up knowing, somehow, that when I left that room, that was the last time I would see the room again. I truly felt it in my bones. I don't know how. I had never seen John Lennon up to that point. I only knew that he was in the Dakota. But I somehow knew that this was it, this was the day. So I laid out on the dresser at the hotel room . . . just a tableau [arrangement] of everything that was important in my life. So it would say, 'Look, this is me. Probably, this is the real me. This is my past and I'm going, gone to another place.'"

Was this tableau a final message to the world from Chapman? Did he expect that he would be killed after he assassinated Lennon? Did he plan to kill himself, as he'd tried to do in the past? Or was he just trying to leave a record of his favorite parts of himself, before the police and the media broadcast his crime to the world?

No one but Chapman knows for certain. For the moment, he was simply headed back to the Dakota. But along the way, he made a brief stop at a bookstore, where he bought a copy of *The Catcher in the Rye* and a pen. Standing on the sidewalk outside the store, he wrote, "This is my statement" inside the book's front cover.

With the treasured book in hand, Chapman headed onward to the Dakota building. There he waited and watched for Lennon.

A DAY IN THE LIFE

While Chapman stood outside the Dakota, John went about a full schedule of work and errands. That day he and Yoko had a photo shoot with celebrity photographer Annie Leibovitz. She was taking pictures of John for an upcoming cover of *Rolling Stone* magazine.

Fans commonly hung out around the Dakota waiting to get autographs from the celebrities who lived there. While Chapman waited outside for Lennon, he spoke with fans hoping to meet the iconic singer.

ccording to Chapman, John was not the only person he had thought about assassinating. He had a list of other famous people he had considered. The list included television talk-show host and comedian Johnny Carson, actress Elizabeth Taylor, and Jackie Onassis (John F. Kennedy's famous widow).

Leibovitz had photographed John before. But this day's session would be a little different. John insisted that Yoko be on the cover with him. Leibovitz knew that her editor at the magazine wasn't keen on the idea. Most of the public still wasn't crazy about Yoko. Leibovitz took some photos of John alone. But she also honored John's wishes and took photos of the couple.

The resulting images included a photograph that would become iconic. It shows John nude, curled around a fully clothed Yoko, kissing her cheek. Yoko remembered the shoot fondly. "We were feeling comfortable because it was Annie, whom we respected and trusted, so John seemed not to have any problem taking off his clothes. John and I were hugging each other, feeling a bit giggly and up."

Around one in the afternoon, John and Yoko had another appointment. Dave Sholin, a San Francisco-based radio producer, came to the Dakota to interview the couple. They talked about their upcoming album and about life. Sholin recalled that John was in high spirits during the interview, which lasted for a couple of hours. "He couldn't have been any more upbeat, any more excited . . . about what was to come and what he wanted to do," Sholin said.

John was brimming with optimism about the new album, his life, his family, and his future. About the album, he said, "We feel like [*Double Fantasy*] is just a start. . . . I feel like nothing has ever happened before today." John went on, "I consider that my work won't be finished until I'm dead and buried, and I hope that's a long, long time."

THIN ICE

At about five in the afternoon, John and Yoko left the Dakota. They headed to the recording studio. The song that the couple would focus on in that session was a Yoko number titled "Walking on Thin Ice."

As John walked from the Dakota to a waiting limousine, Chapman approached the man he'd come to kill. The loaded gun hung heavily in his coat pocket. As John and Yoko strode down the Dakota's walk, Chapman stepped toward the former Beatle and stretched out his arm.

But Chapman did not draw the gun. Instead, he held out *Double Fantasy*. Chapman later recalled the encounter. "I . . . stopped Mr. Lennon and said, 'John, would you sign my album?' And he was very, very kind to me, very pleasant and he said, 'Sure.' And then wrote his name and signed 1980 underneath his name."

While John granted an autograph to Chapman, photographer Paul Goresh was standing nearby. He often waited outside the Dakota, hoping to get a picture of John that he could sell to a newspaper or magazine. That day, he snapped a shot of John and Chapman as John signed the album.

Without realizing it, John had met his assassin—and had escaped without harm. According to Chapman, things might have stayed that way. He says he fought an inner battle after receiving the signature. He told himself that he could just go home, taking the signed album with him as a cherished souvenir.

But Chapman lost the battle. He later described the force of his obsession. "It was like a runaway train. There was no

WORTH A THOUSAND WORDS

hotographer Paul Goresh did earn fame and fortune—at least briefly—with a picture he took of John Lennon. But his success was tainted by tragedy. The photo Goresh snapped of John and Chapman, as John signed Chapman's copy of *Double Fantasy* the day he was assassinated, soon became a hot item. Goresh is reported to have sold the image to the *New York Daily News* in 1980 for $10,000.

12-page pullout on John Lennon—Page 27

DAILY ⊚ NEWS

★★★★ 25¢   NEW YORK, WEDNESDAY, DECEMBER 10, 1980   Mostly sunny, windy, 20s. Details p. 70

No Lennon funeral

YOKO: PRAY FOR HIS SOUL
Page 3

EXCLUSIVE!

John Lennon and his accused killer

John Lennon signs autograph for Mark Chapman, his suspected killer, on Monday. PAUL GORESH/DAILY NEWS ©COPYRIGHT 1980 NEW YORK NEWS INC.

Paul Goresh's photo of John signing Chapman's copy of *Double Fantasy* appeared in the *New York Daily News* on December 10, 1980, two days after Lennon's death.

stopping it. Nothing could have stopped me from doing what I did. Not prayer, not my will, not the devil, not any man, not any bodyguard."

At 10:50 P.M., Chapman was still standing outside the Dakota. John and Yoko pulled up in a limousine. They stepped out onto the sidewalk, with Yoko walking a little bit ahead of John. Yoko passed Chapman first, and then John walked by him.

"There was no emotion, there was no anger, there was nothing, dead silence in the brain, dead cold quiet," Chapman later recalled. "[John] walked up, he looked at me, I tell you the man was going to be dead in less than five minutes, and he looked at me, I looked at him. He walked past me, and then I heard [a voice] in my head [that] said, 'Do it, do it, do it,' over and over again, saying 'Do it, do it, do it, do it,' like that. I pulled the gun out of my pocket, I handed [it] over to my left hand, I don't remember aiming, I must have done, but I don't remember drawing the bead or whatever you call it. And I just pulled the trigger steady five times."

The shots rang out. John, bleeding heavily from the shots to his back, staggered away from Chapman. He managed to climb six steps leading to a small room by the Dakota's entrance. Moaning, "I'm shot," he collapsed face down on the floor.

11:07 P.M.

Chapman made no attempt to flee the crime scene. Steve Spiro and Peter Cullen were the first police officers to respond. Cullen was surprised by Chapman's appearance.

Police hold back crowds at the Dakota on December 9, 1980. Fans quickly flocked to the Dakota after hearing of John's death.

"He looked like a guy who worked in a bank, an office," Cullen said. "Not a loser or anything, just a guy out there trying to earn a living. I remember taking a look at him and saying, 'Why? What did you do here?' He really had no answer for it. He did say several times, 'I'm sorry I gave you guys all this trouble.'"

John was so badly injured that the police officers placed him gently into the back of a squad car and sped to Roosevelt Hospital. There was no time to wait for an ambulance.

Dr. Stephan G. Lynn was running the Roosevelt emergency room that night. John's heart had stopped by the time he arrived at the hospital. Lynn did everything he could to save John's life, including opening John's chest and trying to massage the heart back to life. But the damage was too great. Four of Chapman's five shots had hit John. Two had struck him in the back, while the other two had hit his shoulder. The doctor described the grim trauma the hollow-point bullets had done to John's body. "All the major blood vessels leaving the heart were a mush, and there was no way to fix it."

After a short, intense, and doomed battle to save John, Lynn admitted defeat. He pronounced John dead at 11:07 P.M. "All the nurses broke out in tears," Lynn recalled. "There was a sense we had all just witnessed a major event."

CAUSE OF **DEATH**

ew York's chief medical examiner, Dr. Elliot M. Gross, performed John's autopsy on December 9, 1980. After the exam, he confirmed that John had died of shock and massive loss of blood. The four bullets did major damage inside John's body, including to his left lung as well as a major artery, and doctors were unable to stop the bleeding. In addition, shock can cause the body's tissues and organs to receive inadequate amounts of blood and oxygen.

Lynn's role in the tragedy wasn't over yet. He still had to break the news to Yoko. "When I told her, she said: 'You're lying; it can't be true. He's not dead. I don't believe you.' She threw herself down on the floor and began banging her head on the ground. I was afraid we'd have a second patient."

At the hospital, an ABC television station employee overheard the doctor talking to Yoko. He quickly called ABC with the news. Howard Cosell interrupted his coverage of the *Monday Night Football* broadcast to announce John's death. From that moment, the story traveled quickly. DJs on radio stations around the country announced John's death to their listeners. Friends called one another to share their shock.

Family friend Elliot Mintz was in Los Angeles, California, when he heard the news that John had been shot. He quickly caught a flight to New York, hoping for the best. But his hope was short-lived. He recalled, "Just after take-off, I was sitting alone when the cockpit door opened. A stewardess appeared with tears streaming down her face." Mintz learned then that his fears had come true. Other people, stricken by the news, also headed to New York. Soon after seventeen-year-old Julian heard of his father's murder, he boarded a plane from England.

On December 9, Yoko released a short statement to the public. It read in part, "John loved and prayed for the human race. Please pray the same for him. Love, Yoko and Sean."

CHAPTER FIVE

POSTMORTEM

Judge Dennis Edwards: Tell the court in your own words, what it is you did on December 8, 1980.

Mark David Chapman: I intended to kill John Lennon and that night I drew a pistol from my pocket, proceeded to shoot him with intent to kill him.

—MARK CHAPMAN'S TRIAL TRANSCRIPT,
JUNE 22, 1981

As the world learned of John's death, Chapman became the world's most famous murder suspect. Upon his arrest, police whisked him to New York's 20th Precinct police station. About two hours after the murder, about one in the morning on December 9, Chapman wrote a statement of confession. The following is an excerpt:

I never wanted to hurt anybody my friends will tell you that. I have two big parts in me the big part is very kind the children I worked with will tell you that. I have a small part in me that cannot understand the big world and what goes on in it. I did not want to kill anybody and I really don't know why I did it. I fought against the small part for a long time. But for a few seconds the small part won. I asked God to help me but we are responsible for our own actions. I have nothing against John Lennon or anything he has done in the way of music or personal beliefs. I came to New York about five weeks ago from Hawaii and the big part of me did not want me to shoot John. I went back to Hawaii and tryed [tried] to get rid of my small part but I couldn't. I then returned to New York on [Saturday] December [6], 1980 I checked into the YMCA on 62 Street [63rd Street]. I stayed one night. Then I went to the Sheraton Center 7th Ave. Then this morning I went to the book store and bought The Catcher in the Rye. I'm sure the large part of me is Holden Caulfield who is the main person in the book. The small part of me must be the Devil. I went to the building its called the Dakota. I stayed there until he [Lennon] came out and asked him to sign my album. At that point my big part won and I wanted to go back to my hotel, but I couldn't. I waited until he came back. He came in a car. Yoko past [passed] first and I said hello, I didn't want to hurt her. Then John came, looked at me and past me. I took the gun from my coat pocket and fired at him. I can't believe I could do that. I just stood there clutching the book. I didn't want to run away. I don't know what happened to the gun, I just remember Jose [a doorman at the Dakota] kicking it away. Jose was crying and telling me to please leave. I felt so sorry for Jose. Then the police came and told me to put my hands on the wall and cuffed me.

Early on the morning of December 9, police officers faced a challenge. They had to take Chapman to court, where he would be arraigned (formally charged with a crime). But the media was hungry for a glimpse of the killer. A crowd had gathered in and around the station. The police were concerned about Chapman's safety, fearing that a distraught Lennon fan might try to harm or kill him.

The police strapped a bulletproof vest to Chapman and allowed him to cover his head with a coat to hide his face. Then they hustled him through the police station's hallways and to Manhattan's nearby Criminal Courts Building. There, the court

Chapman *(center with coat over head)* is escorted out of the police station on his way to the Criminal Courts Building in New York City on December 9, 1980.

charged him with second-degree murder. In New York, second-degree murder is the most serious charge for the murder of a person who is not a law enforcement officer.

That same day, Chapman met his court-appointed defense lawyer, Herbert Adlerberg. But Adlerberg did not stay with the case very long. After receiving multiple death threats, he stepped down as Chapman's defense. Jonathan Marks took his place.

This courtroom sketch shows Mark David Chapman's arraignment on December 9 for the murder of John Lennon.

HEAD CASE

One big question hung over the upcoming murder trial: was Chapman sane? Seeking the answer would occupy the lawyers on both sides of Chapman's case in the days and weeks to come.

The first expert to weigh in on the matter was Dr. Naomi Goldstein of New York City's Bellevue Hospital Center. On the evening of December 9, police escorted Chapman to Bellevue's psychiatric wing. In a small and heavily guarded room, Goldstein interviewed Chapman and tried to determine his mental state. Her notes included the following description: "Speech coherent, relevant, and logical. No evidence [of] hallucination or delusions. Clinical evaluation reveals a pleasant, generally cooperative young man."

Despite Goldstein's assessment of Chapman as a mild-mannered man, doctors at

Bellevue placed Chapman on suicide watch. They worried that like many other murder suspects, Chapman might try to take his own life rather than face justice for his crime. A guard checked on him every fifteen minutes to make sure he didn't harm himself or try to escape.

Officials then took Chapman to New York's Rikers Island jail complex. He didn't get a regular cell at Rikers. Worried that other inmates might attack him for killing the popular Lennon, prison officials isolated Chapman in the prison hospital. Chapman was frightened, especially after seeing a threat against him written on a wall. He went on a two-day hunger strike, refusing to eat for fear that his food was poisoned.

Goldstein wasn't the last doctor to evaluate Chapman. On January 6, 1981, Chapman and Marks appeared in court, and Chapman pled not guilty by reason of insanity. The judge at the hearing, Herbert Altman, agreed to Marks's request for mental health experts to examine his client. Altman approved the hiring of two psychiatrists and one clinical psychologist.

PUBLIC **ENEMY**

In the days after Chapman's arrest, law enforcement authorities were deeply concerned about his safety. While Chapman was at Bellevue, workers painted the windows of his room black to prevent any attempted shootings from nearby buildings. Even decades later, Chapman may not be entirely safe in prison. For most of his time at Attica prison, he has been in solitary confinement. Usually, inmates are in solitary confinement because they are dangerous. Chapman did have a few violent outbursts—raving, shouting, and destroying things in his cell—early in his prison term. But mostly, he has been a calm, cooperative prisoner. So why the solitary confinement? Certain types of criminals often face threats from others within the prison walls. For example, those who commit particularly antisocial crimes, such as child abuse, are frequently singled out for violence. Because of the high-profile nature of Chapman's crime and because many people of many backgrounds loved and admired Lennon, prison officials worry that Chapman's fellow inmates could be a danger to him.

MIND **GAMES**

Although many psychiatric experts have interviewed Chapman over the years, no conclusive diagnosis of Chapman's mental health has ever been made. Chapman himself has said that he believes he is schizophrenic, and some doctors agree. Schizophrenia is a mental illness that often involves hallucinations, delusions, and a general lack of connection to reality. Chapman's stories of the Little People, for example, seem to fit the diagnosis of schizophrenia. Other people—including author Jack Jones, who has interviewed Chapman many times—label Chapman a sociopath. A sociopath is a person with a serious personality disorder, the symptoms of which include antisocial behavior, a lack of conscience, and a lack of normal human emotion. Still others believe that Chapman is sane but very good at mimicking the signs of certain mental illnesses—perhaps to puzzle the legal authorities.

Chapman spoke to one psychiatrist about the Little People of his childhood. He claimed that after he had gone many years without seeing the Little People, they had returned while he was living in Hawaii. He also confessed that he had worshipped Satan at times. Marks also brought famous psychiatrist Dr. Lee Salk to see Chapman. Chapman told Salk that he'd fantasized about killing his father. "I was going to break into his house, and get him in his room alone, and put a gun to him and tell him what I thought about him," he said. "And then I was going to blow his head off."

Marks planned to base his defense case on the claim that Chapman was not sane at the time of the murder. Knowing this, the prosecution team—led by Allen Sullivan—called on its own medical experts to assess Chapman's state of mind. But none of the mental health experts—on either side of the case—could agree on a diagnosis.

As it turned out, it didn't matter. About two weeks before the scheduled trial, Chapman decided, on his own, to change his plea to guilty. That sudden change made a jury trial unnecessary. Marks, who had invested so many hours in building a

CLOSE TO **A KILLER**

hen details of Mark David Chapman's personal life began to reach reporters, they wanted to talk to the people who knew him best. His wife, Gloria Chapman, said, "Being a Beatles fan, I mourn the death of John Lennon." She also expressed her sympathy for John's family. "I'm very, very sorry that this had to happen. Sorry for Yoko and her son, Sean, and that her husband had to die." But she also said that she forgave her husband. "I can't recall when I've not forgiven Mark," she said.

Chapman's mother responded differently. "This thing hit me totally out of the blue," she said. "It just never seemed real. It seems like fiction. . . . That's why I suppose in some ways it would be hard for me to see Mark, because then it would probably be more real."

Chapman's father said simply, "It's just like [he's] a different person than I used to know."

defense case, was not happy about the decision. He believed he had a good chance of successfully arguing that Chapman was not guilty of murder, by reason of insanity. He urged his client to reconsider, but Chapman refused to change his mind. He said that God had told him to plead guilty.

SENTENCED

On June 22, 1981, Chapman attended a court hearing to assess the state of his mental health so that his sentence could be determined. The judge, Dennis Edwards, wanted to decide for himself whether Chapman understood what it meant to change his plea. Edwards asked Chapman a series of questions about his crime and about his plea. Having heard the answers, the judge believed that Chapman did understand his actions and their consequences. Chapman's sentencing took place two months later, on August 24. At that hearing, Marks and prosecutor Allen Sullivan both spoke before Judge Edwards, who had come to a decision about Chapman's sentence. "[Chapman] wanted to steal someone else's fame," Sullivan argued. "He got what he wanted." Marks maintained his original argument that Chapman was not sane when he murdered Lennon.

Judge Edwards asked Chapman if he wanted to say anything before hearing the sentence. In response, Chapman stood and read from *The Catcher in the Rye*. He chose to read Holden Caulfield's vision of himself as the "catcher in the rye." Chapman read aloud, "Anyway, I keep picturing all these little kids playing some game in this big field of rye and all. Thousands of little kids, and nobody's around—nobody big, I mean—except me. And I'm standing on the edge of some crazy cliff. What I have to do, I have to catch everybody if they start to go over the cliff—I mean if they're running and they don't look where they're going I have to come out from somewhere and catch them. That's all I do all day. I'd just be the catcher in the rye and all."

In a statement before reading the sentence, Edwards said, "I disagree with the defense attorney's suggestion that it [the murder] is . . . an act of a person who is insane. It may well not be a crime committed for the classic motives, revenge or for money; but it was, as the district attorney carefully pointed out, an intentional crime. It was a crime contemplated, planned and executed by an individual fully aware of the situation and the consequences of his conduct. . . . There is no doubt in the court's judgment that he is to be held accountable and responsible for his knowing, voluntary, and intelligent act."

Edwards then gave the sentence. "Mark David Chapman is sentenced to State Correctional Facility for a minimum jail sentence of twenty years and a maximum jail sentence of life."

With his punishment determined, Chapman went to Attica Correctional Facility in Attica, New York. There he took up residence in a small cell. And there he would remain for decades.

PAROLE HEARINGS

Chapman first became eligible for parole [early release from prison] in 2000. Before his parole hearing took place, Yoko sent a letter to the parole board requesting that they deny freedom to her husband's killer. She wrote, "John Lennon . . . brought light

Attica Correctional Facility in Attica, New York, holds more than two thousand convicted criminals, including Mark David Chapman.

and hope to the whole world with his words and music. . . . When the 'subject' pulled the trigger . . . It was as though the light went out for a moment and darkness prevailed." She also cited fear for herself and both of John's sons if Chapman were to be released.

In October 2000, Chapman appeared before the parole board. During the fifty-minute meeting, Chapman said, "I'd like to take the opportunity to apologize to Mrs. Lennon [Ono]. I've thought about what it's like in her mind to be there that night, to see the blood, hear the screams, to be up all night with the Beatles music playing through her apartment window."

He went on, "I feel that I see John Lennon now not as a celebrity. I did then. I saw him as a cardboard cutout on an album cover. I was very young and stupid, and you get caught up in the media and the records and the music. And now . . . I've come to grips with the fact that John Lennon was a person. This has nothing to do with being a Beatle or a celebrity or famous. He was breathing, and I knocked him right off his feet. . . . I don't have a leg to stand on

NYS DOCS

75
72
69

81A3860
CHAPMAN, MARK D
6'0" 200lbs
DATE 12/22/2003

57

Sex - MALE   Race - WHITE   Hair - BALD   Eyes - BLUE

This mug shot of Mark David Chapman was taken in 2003.

because I took his right out from under him, and he bled to death." The parole board agreed and denied parole.

Chapman has been eligible for parole once every two years since 2000. Each time, the parole board has decided that he will remain in prison. In September 2010, the parole board declared that releasing Chapman would be "incompatible with the welfare of the community."

Some observers believe that part of the reason Chapman is still imprisoned is actually for his own safety. Over the years, he has received many death threats. If Chapman were ever released from prison, he could be at risk.

Chapman does have a few visitors at Attica. Gloria sometimes goes to see him. Several mental health experts have spoken with him since his imprisonment. And a handful of reporters and writers have interviewed him. Opinions about him continue to differ widely. Some people who meet him find him chillingly sane, while others believe that he is mentally ill.

RHYME AND REASON

According to Chapman, on the night of his arrest, one of the police officers guarding him had asked, "Mark, why'd you do it?" Chapman recalled, "I remember what I said to him. I said, without hesitation, 'I can't understand what's going on in the world and what it's become.'"

This question of "why" continues to haunt many observers, writers, and heartbroken fans—not to mention John's friends and family. Analysts have proposed a few ideas. One theory relies on the belief that Chapman is—or was at the moment of the shooting— mentally ill. It suggests that Chapman

truly believed that he would become Holden Caulfield by killing a man he'd come to view as a "phony." Another theory is that Chapman was sane and wanted fame and attention. He knew he would get both by murdering a celebrity. This was the explanation the prosecution lawyer offered, and many others agree.

One puzzling factor has been that Chapman's motives, as he describes them, seem to change. Even three decades after the crime, not everything is clear about why Chapman shot John Lennon on December 8, 1980. For example, while sitting in prison awaiting a trial that never happened, he said, "The reason I killed John Lennon was to gain prominence to promote the reading of J. D. Salinger's *The Catcher in the Rye*. I'm not saying I'm a messiah [savior] or anything like that. If you read the book and if you understand my past . . . you will see that I am indeed 'The Catcher in the Rye' of this generation."

Later, in a 1992 interview from Attica with television journalist Barbara Walters, he claimed that celebrity was his goal.

Conspiracy theories abound when it comes to John Lennon's murder. John's own son Sean has said he believes that there was more to the crime than was apparent. Years afterward, he said, "[My dad] . . . was very dangerous to the [U.S.] government. If he had said 'Bomb the White House tomorrow,' there would have been 10,000 people who would have done it. The pacifist revolutionaries are historically killed by the government, and anybody who thinks Mark Chapman was just some crazy guy who killed my dad for his own personal interest is insane or very naive. It was in the best interest of the United States to have my dad killed."

Sean's belief may stem from the anger of a grieving son. But he is not alone in his suspicions. Not long after John's death, British lawyer and writer Fenton Bresler began digging into the case. He wasn't sure that Chapman acted alone. Bresler spent more than five years investigating the details of John's assassination. In his 1989 book, *Who Killed John Lennon?* he suggested that the U.S. Central Intelligence Agency (CIA) may have "programmed"—or used some form of mental control on—Chapman to get him to assassinate John. (The CIA is a U.S. government agency that handles international intelligence, or strategic information.) The reason for such a plan, Bresler suggests, could have been to prevent John from influencing U.S. politics.

A different theory also involves the CIA. On the night that Chapman killed John, the doorman working at the Dakota was Jose Perdomo. Perdomo, who was born in Cuba, opposed Fidel Castro, Cuba's dictator. The CIA sometimes hired Cuban exiles as agents, and some people think that Perdomo was hired to kill John. Others believe that Chapman himself was not even the killer but was framed and somehow convinced—or forced—to take the blame.

No proof exists to support any of these conspiracy theories, however. Most people who have seriously studied the case dismiss them as pure fantasy.

Chapman told Walters, "I thought by killing [Lennon] I would acquire his fame." And at his 2000 parole hearing, he said, "I was feeling like I was worthless. . . . I felt like nothing, and I felt if I shot him, I would become something . . . that's why I shot Mr. Lennon."

But at other times, he has insisted that a desire for fame had nothing to do with his actions. At one point, in a letter to British lawyer, journalist, and author Fenton Bresler, who had written about John's murder, Chapman expressed his own confusion. He wrote, "The reasons for Mr. Lennon's death are very complex and I am still trying to sort them out emotionally myself."

In the end, the world will never know exactly what was going through Chapman's mind leading up to John Lennon's assassination. John's friends, family, and fans can only take some comfort in knowing that Chapman has lived in a small cell at Attica for more than a quarter of a century. Although a formal jury trial never took place, justice was done. John's killer remains behind bars.

CHAPTER SIX
"STRAWBERRY FIELDS FOREVER"

Death alone doesn't extinguish a flame
and a spirit like John.

—YOKO ONO, 1981

While lawyers and psychiatrists and judges interviewed, examined, and
sentenced Mark David Chapman, John Lennon's family, friends, and fans
grieved. In the days and weeks after John's death, words of sorrow and remembrance
poured out from some of the world's most famous people.

John's fellow Beatles were among the earliest to speak out. Paul McCartney said,
"I am deeply shocked and saddened at the tragic death. John was a great man who
will be greatly missed but remembered for his unique contribution to art, music and
world peace." George Harrison commented, "After all we went through together
I had and still have great love and respect for him. I am shocked and stunned."
Ringo Starr issued no statement, but he flew to New York to be with Yoko and Sean.
The Beatles' producer, George Martin, said, "John's death made me very angry at
the violence, that a violent world should do this to one of the great people of our
time. . . . [John] was a true original, with a zany sense of humor that could elevate the
meanest of spirits. . . . He'll be missed."

Political figures also shared their reactions. "[John Lennon's] spirit, the spirit of
the Beatles—brash and earnest, ironic and idealistic all at once—became the spirit

Ringo Starr *(right)* and his girlfriend, Barbara Bach *(center)*, leave the Dakota after visiting Yoko shortly after John's death.

of the whole generation," said President Jimmy Carter. "It is especially poignant that John Lennon has died by violence, though he had long campaigned for peace."

MOURNING A TRAGEDY

Fans maintained their vigil outside the Dakota for several days after John's death. They also sent letters to the Dakota apartment, pouring out their love and admiration for John. At the gate of the Dakota, people left flowers, notes, and pictures.

The mourning reached well beyond New York. In Liverpool, many people honored John's memory by leaving flowers near the former site of the Cavern. Fans also grieved in Hamburg, where the Beatles had played some of their earliest concerts. In the Netherlands, the Amsterdam Hilton—the site of John and Yoko's honeymoon bed-in in 1969—offered its own tribute. On the night of December 9, 1980, the hotel turned out all its lights except those of the suite where the bed-in had taken place.

Record stores across the United States and around the world became impromptu meeting places for stricken fans. Some shops sold out of Beatles and Lennon records in a matter of hours.

On December 14, 1980, the moment of silence that Yoko had called for took place. The ten-minute vigil began at two in the afternoon in New York, which was seven in the evening in Britain. Around the globe, hundreds of thousands of people joined in the tribute to John. In New York City, an estimated one hundred thousand people came together in Central Park. About twenty thousand gathered in Liverpool. Thousands more assembled across the United States and in countries including France, Spain, Germany, and Australia. During those ten minutes, many radio stations also went silent in John's memory.

Fans gather in New York City's Central Park on December 14, 1980, for a vigil to celebrate John's memory.

On January 22, 1981, the photo of John and Yoko that Annie Leibovitz had taken on the day of John's death appeared on the cover of *Rolling Stone*. Inside the magazine were articles about John's life, music, and death.

Meanwhile, Yoko struggled to adjust to life as John Lennon's widow. She turned to her work—and to music—for comfort. In June 1981, she released an album titled *Season of Glass*. Its front cover shows the bloodied glasses that John still had on his face after Chapman shot him. In the picture, the glasses sit on a desk by a window in the Dakota, next to a half full glass of water. Beyond is a view of Central Park and the city's skyline. Some fans criticized Yoko for showing John's glasses, calling the album cover morbid and disrespectful. But Yoko said, "John would have approved, and I will explain why. I wanted the whole world to be reminded of what happened. People are offended by the glasses and the blood? The glasses are a tiny part of what happened. If people can't stomach the glasses, I'm sorry. There was a dead body. There was blood. . . . That's the reality. I want people to face up to what happened. He did not commit suicide. He was *killed*."

The year 1981 also brought recognition for John's last official album. *Double Fantasy* won the Grammy (the U.S. music industry's highest honor) for Album of the Year. Yoko and Sean accepted the award on John's behalf.

IN MEMORIAM

On October 9, 1985—what would have been John's forty-fifth birthday—New York City formally opened a garden in Central Park dedicated to his memory. The garden is named Strawberry Fields, after the Beatles song "Strawberry Fields Forever." It lies just across the street from the Dakota, where Yoko and Sean still lived at the time. About the memorial, Yoko said, "I didn't want a funeral for John because I felt that his spirit lives. Instead, this garden—it's a living memorial."

Italy contributed this mosaic to Strawberry Fields, the garden in New York's Central Park that celebrates Lennon.

To embody the spirit of international peace, Yoko invited countries around the world to contribute plants to the garden. In all, Strawberry Fields contains plant life representing more than 150 different nations. For example, the Netherlands offered daffodils, Canada sent maple trees, and Israel contributed cedars. Italy sent a black-and-white mosaic artwork that spells the word "Imagine." This piece has become a focal point of the 2.5-acre (1-hectare) garden.

Tributes to John Lennon continue to flow from fans all over the world. Hundreds visit the Strawberry Fields memorial in Central Park every year, especially on John's birthday and on the anniversary of his death. People have also gathered there in the wake of other deaths or tragedies, such as after the terrorist attacks of September 11, 2001, and after George Harrison died in November of the same year.

Statues of John and monuments to his memory dot the globe. Not surprisingly, several statues stand in Liverpool, including one on the street where the Cavern used to be. Other tributes include a statue in Havana, Cuba, in the city's John Lennon Park. Statues also stand in several cities in Spain, as well as in Lima, Peru.

In 2002 Liverpool renamed its airport the Liverpool John Lennon Airport. The airport adopted the slogan, "above us only sky." The line comes from John's song "Imagine."

In 2007 a memorial called the Imagine Peace Tower opened in Iceland. Located on a tiny island off Iceland's western coast, the tower is built from a wishing well. From the

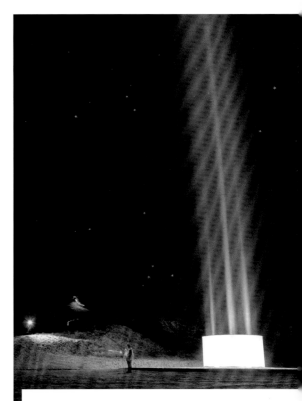

The Imagine Peace Tower on Vidential Island, near Reykjavik, lights up the Icelandic sky with its message of peace.

well, a huge and brilliant beam of light shines up into the sky. On the base of the tower, the words "Imagine Peace" are engraved in twenty-four languages, from Italian, Russian, and Finnish to Korean, Swahili, and Hindi. Each year, the tower lights up on October 9, John's birthday, and remains lit until December 8. Yoko said of the memorial, "Contrasting the two symbolic dates . . . gives an understanding of the shortness of life, and eternity of the spirit."

THE LEGEND LIVES ON

John Lennon was far from perfect. Many people speak of his brilliance, his passion, and his idealism. He could be gentle and kind, and his wit was famous. But he also struggled with addictions to drugs, and he sometimes drank too heavily. He was prone to anger and harsh words. And some feel that he didn't treat his first wife or his first son as well as he should have. He was complex, changeable, and deeply charismatic.

But John's flaws and his contradictions seemed only to have made him more fascinating. As Paul McCartney put it, "John was a great guy, but part of his greatness was that he wasn't a saint." Three decades after John's death, the public's desire for information about him remains strong. Dozens of books have sought new insights and new details about John, his life, his music, and his murder. Many films—both documentaries and dramas—have also delved into the story.

That story changes depending on who tells it. As he did in life, John Lennon continues to create controversy. But his music and his writing endure as testaments to a talented and complicated man.

THE FAMILY **BUSINESS**

John's legacy lives on through his two sons. Both Julian and Sean have followed in their father's footsteps by pursuing music careers as singers and songwriters.

Julian released his first album, *Valotte*, in 1984, to good reviews. He followed with four more studio albums. In addition, he has branched out into other artistic fields. For example, he produced a 2006 documentary titled *Whaledreamers*, about a native Australian people and their spiritual connection to whales. Julian also contributed a song to the film's sound track.

Sean's career has also involved movies. He has composed music for six films, has cowritten others, and has produced still others. He also has pursued a recording career. Sean has released three solo albums, the first of which was called *Into the Sun*, as well as singing backup on other artists' albums and playing bass with the Japanese girl band Cibo Matto.

Sean *(left)* and Julian *(right)* Lennon and their mothers attend a showing of Julian's photography in New York City in 2010. Both of John's sons have made careers in music and the arts.

TIMELINE

1940 John Winston Lennon is born in Liverpool, England, on October 9.

1951 J. D. Salinger's classic novel, *The Catcher in the Rye*, is published.

1952 John Lennon enters Quarry Bank High School.

1955 John Lennon's uncle George dies suddenly on June 5. Mark David Chapman is born in Fort Worth, Texas, on May 10.

1957 John Lennon and several friends form a skiffle group called the Quarrymen. That summer John meets Paul McCartney at a Quarrymen gig. McCartney soon joins the band. That fall John begins attending the Liverpool College of Art.

1958 In February George Harrison joins the Quarrymen as a guitarist. On July 15, a car driven by an off-duty police officer hits Julia Lennon. She dies instantly.

1960 The Quarrymen tour Scotland in May. That winter the band books an engagement in Hamburg, Germany. Before heading to Germany, the band renames itself the Beatles.

1961 The Beatles become regular performers at Liverpool's Cavern Club in March. Brian Epstein first sees the Beatles there in November.

1962 Epstein secures a record deal for the Beatles. Ringo Starr signs on as the Beatles' drummer in August. Later that month, John marries Cynthia Powell.

1963 The Lennons' son, John Charles Julian Lennon, is born on April 8.

1964 The Beatles perform in the United States on the *Ed Sullivan Show* in February, attracting an estimated 73 million viewers. John's first book, *In His Own Write*, is published in April. The Beatles' first movie, *A Hard Day's Night*, is released in the summer.

1965 The Beatles' film *Help!* is released in July. The Beatles play a legendary show at New York City's Shea Stadium on August 15.

1966 John's remarks about the Beatles being more popular than Jesus Christ become controversial in the United States. The Beatles play their final live concert in San Francisco on August 29. John meets Japanese American artist Yoko Ono in November.

1967 *Sgt. Pepper's Lonely Hearts Club Band* is released in May. In August Beatles manager Brian Epstein dies of an accidental drug overdose.

1968 John and Cynthia Lennon separate in August. On November 22, the Beatles release a record that comes to be known as the *White Album*. One week later, John and Yoko release their first album, *Unfinished Music No. 1: Two Virgins*.

1969 John and Yoko form the Plastic Ono Band. On March 20, John and Yoko are married in Gibraltar. Later that month, they hold their first "bed-in" at the Amsterdam Hilton in the Netherlands. In September John says that he is leaving the Beatles. On October 15, the Moratorium to End the War in Vietnam takes place in cities around the United States.

1971 John releases the solo album *Imagine*. John and Yoko move to New York City. In December John and Yoko go to Ann Arbor, Michigan, to participate in a rally to free antiwar activist John Sinclair. Around this time, Chapman first reads *The Catcher in the Rye*.

1972 John learns that he is facing deportation from the United States. Chapman works at a YMCA summer camp in Decatur, Georgia.

1973 The Watergate scandal rocks Richard Nixon's presidency. Chapman graduates from high school.

1975 The Vietnam War ends. In the summer, Chapman travels to Beirut, Lebanon, as part of his job with the YMCA. On October 9, Yoko gives birth to Sean Taro Ono Lennon.

1976 In August Chapman works with refugees at a YMCA-run camp in Fort Chaffee, Arkansas. Chapman goes on to enroll at Covenant College in Lookout Mountain, Georgia.

1977 Chapman moves to Hawaii. Later that year, he attempts suicide. When his attempt fails, he checks into the mental health ward of Castle Memorial Hospital. He goes on to get a job there.

1978 Chapman takes a six-week trip around the world. While planning his trip, he meets travel agent Gloria Abe. They begin a romantic relationship.

1979 Chapman and Gloria Abe marry in June. Later that year, Chapman begins behaving erratically. He drinks heavily and becomes abusive toward Gloria.

1980 In late October, Chapman travels to New York intending to kill John but returns to Hawaii without having seen him. John and Yoko release *Double Fantasy* on November 17. Chapman returns to New York on December 6. At 10:50 P.M. on December 8, Chapman shoots John in front of the Dakota building. John is pronounced dead at 11:07 P.M.

1981 Mark David Chapman pleads not guilty to the murder of John Lennon by reason of insanity, on January 6. In June Chapman changes his plea to guilty. In June Yoko releases an album *Season of Glass,* showing John's bloody glasses on the cover. On August 24, Chapman is sentenced to a minimum of twenty years to life in prison.

1985 Strawberry Fields, a garden dedicated to John's memory, opens in New York's Central Park.

1998 Sean Ono Lennon releases his first solo album, *Into the Sun*. Julian Lennon releases his fifth solo album, *Photograph Smile*.

2010 Chapman is denied parole for the sixth time. The year marks the thirtieth anniversary of John's death—and the occasion of what would have been his seventieth birthday.

2011 The Rock and Roll Hall of Fame in Cleveland, Ohio, updates and improves its Beatles exhibit with help and advice from Yoko Ono, Ringo Starr's team, and George Harrison's widow.

WHO'S **WHO?**

GEORGE HARRISON (1943–2001) Born in Liverpool, Harrison was a classmate of Paul McCartney's at the Liverpool Institute. At the age of fifteen, he joined the Quarrymen as the band's lead guitarist. Following the band's breakup, he went on to a successful solo career. In 1988 Harrison became part of the Traveling Wilburys, a so-called supergroup that included Bob Dylan and Tom Petty. His personal life included marriage to model Pattie Boyd in 1966. They later divorced and Harrison married Olivia Trinidad Arias. He and his second wife had one son.

CYNTHIA LENNON (B. 1939) Born Cynthia Powell in Blackpool, England, Cynthia was the youngest of three children. She attended Liverpool's Junior Art School and later the Liverpool Institute of Art, where she met John Lennon. The two married in August 1962. Their son, Julian, was born in April 1963. Their marriage fell apart because of John's drug use and his relationship with Yoko Ono, and the couple divorced in 1968. In 2002 Cynthia married her third husband, Noel Charles, and lives with him in Spain.

JULIA LENNON (1914–1958) John Lennon's mother was born in Liverpool, England, as Julia Stanley. She grew up to be a free-spirited and lively woman with a love of music. She met Alfred Lennon when the two were in their teens. They married in 1938, and Julia gave birth to their son, John Lennon, in 1940. However, the couple split up within a few years. When Julia found herself unprepared to care for John alone, she sent him to live with her sister Mimi. Julia later had three more children, two of them with John Dykins. Julia and John grew closer when John was a teenager, and they enjoyed playing and sharing music. In 1958 she was struck and killed by a car. Several of John Lennon's songs, including "Julia" and "Mother," are about her.

JULIAN LENNON (B. 1963) Julian Lennon was born in Liverpool to Cynthia and John Lennon. He was named after John Lennon's mother, Julia. Julian was born just as the Beatles began to hit the big time. As a result, John was often gone during Julian's early years, and the two never had a close relationship. (However, according to John, the famous Beatles' song "Lucy in the Sky with Diamonds" was inspired by a watercolor painting that young Julian made.) Julian's parents split up when he was five years old, and he and his father had little contact until a period in the early 1970s, when Julian made a trip to see John in the United States. Despite this distant relationship, Julian did follow in his father's steps by pursuing a musical career. He released his first album, *Valotte,* in 1984 and followed with four more studio albums.

SEAN ONO LENNON (B. 1975) Born in New York City, Sean Ono Lennon is the only child of John Lennon and Yoko Ono. Sean attended several private schools, including the Institut Le Rosey in Switzerland. He also briefly went to New York's Columbia University. However, he left college to focus on music. He had expressed an interest in music since boyhood, and even as a child, he appeared on some of Yoko's albums. In 1996 he became a bass player for the girl band Cibo Matto and performed on two of their albums. He has also made several solo albums and composed film scores.

PAUL MCCARTNEY (B. 1942) McCartney
was born in Liverpool. He joined the Quarrymen at the age of fifteen and along with Lennon was one of the two primary songwriters of the Beatles. Following the breakup of the band, McCartney continued to be a prolific musician. In 1971 he formed the successful band Wings. McCartney has also made many solo albums. In 1997 he was knighted in honor of his musical career, formally becoming Sir Paul McCartney. Two years later, he entered the Rock and Roll Hall of Fame. McCartney's personal life includes his 1969 marriage to American photographer Linda Eastman. The couple had four children together and remained married until Linda's death in 1998. In 2002 McCartney married model Heather Mills, with whom he had one child. The couple divorced in 2008. He married Nancy Shevell in 2011. McCartney continues to tour and perform.

YOKO ONO (B. 1933) Yoko was born in
Tokyo, Japan, to a wealthy banking family. After World War II, her family moved to Scarsdale, New York, and Yoko attended Sarah Lawrence College. She became a performing artist, joining the thriving artistic and countercultural scene in New York City. Yoko married twice before meeting Lennon, to Toshi Ichiyanagi in 1956 and to Anthony Cox in 1963. She had a daughter named Kyoko with Cox, who later disappeared with the girl (Yoko and Kyoko reconnected decades later). Meanwhile, Yoko continued to pursue her career as an artist. In 1966 that career took her to England, where she met John Lennon. Since John's death, Yoko has continued her art career and has managed the Lennon estate.

RINGO STARR (B. 1940) Born in Liverpool
as Richard Starkey, young Starr was talented in art, drama, and music. He played in several bands before meeting the Beatles in Hamburg in 1960. Two years later, he formally joined the band as their drummer. Although Starr didn't compose many songs for the group, he did write a few, including "Don't Pass Me By" and "Octopus's Garden." Since the Beatles' breakup, he has released many solo albums. He has also collaborated with other musical artists, as well as participating in charity events. In 1989 Starr formed the All-Starr Band, which over the years has had a changing lineup of many artists and has released several albums. Starr has three children from his first marriage, to Maureen Cox. One of their children, Zak, grew up to become a drummer. Starr has been married to actress Barbara Bach since 1981.

SOURCE NOTES

4 Tom Goldman, "ABC Broadcasts Final 'Monday Night Football,'" NPR.org, December 26, 2005, http://www.npr.org/templates/story/story.php?storyId=5069985 (September 14, 2010).

5 Ibid.

5 Jack Jones, *Let Me Take You Down: Inside the Mind of Mark David Chapman, the Man Who Killed John Lennon* (New York: Villard Books, 1992), xv.

6–7 Yoko Ono, ed., *Memories of John Lennon* (New York: HarperEntertainment, 2005), 211.

9 Fenton Bresler, *Who Killed John Lennon?* (New York: St. Martin's Press, 1989), 61.

9 Ray Coleman, *Lennon: The Definitive Biography* (New York: HarperPerennial, 1992), 98.

11 Ibid., 134.

14 *Life* editors, *Remembering John Lennon: 25 Years Later* (New York: Life Books, 2005), 38.

15 Ben Child, "Beatles Manager Brian Epstein to Be Focus of Fab Four Biopic," Guardian.co.uk, August 26, 2009, http://www.guardian.co.uk/film/2009/aug/26/beatles-brian-epstein-biopic (March 15, 2011).

15 Coleman, *Lennon*, 278–279.

16 Ibid.

16 Ibid.

17 *Imagine: John Lennon*, DVD (Burbank, CA: Warner Home Video, 2005).

18 Ibid.

18 *Time*, "Cinema: Chase & Superchase," Time.com, September 3, 1965, http://www.time.com/time/magazine/article/0,9171,842079,00.html (March 15, 2011).

20 Bresler, *Who Killed John Lennon?*, 61.

21 June Skinner Sawyers, *Read the Beatles: Classic and New Writings on the Beatles, Their Legacy, and Why They Still Matter* (New York: Penguin Books, 2006), 97.

21 Chris Conway, "No, Not Everyone Enjoyed the Show," *New York Times*, June 3, 2007, http://www.nytimes.com/2007/06/03/weekinreview/03basicB.html (March 15, 2010).

21 *The U.S. vs. John Lennon*, DVD (Santa Monica, CA: Lionsgate, 2007).

21–22 Coleman, *Lennon*, 420.

22 Ibid., 433.

24 Ono, *Memories of John Lennon*, 158.

24 Anthony DeCurtis, "His Kind of Shell-Shocked Town," *New York Times*, May 17, 2009, http://www.nytimes.com/2009/05/17/weekinreview/17decurtis.html (March 15, 2010).

26 Coleman, *Lennon*, 583–584.

27 Bresler, *Who Killed John Lennon?*, 61. 26   DeCurtis, "His Kind of Shell-Shocked Town."

29 Jon Wiener, *Come Together: John Lennon in His Time* (Urbana: University of Illinois Press, 1991), 306.

33 Corporation for Public Broadcasting, "The Presidents: LBJ: The Tet Offensive," *American Experience*, 2009, http://www.pbs.org/wgbh/amex/presidents/video/lbj_24.html#v249 (March 21, 2010).

33 *The U.S. vs. John Lennon.*

35 Ibid.

35 Ibid.

35 Coleman, *Lennon*, 578.

36 Wiener, *Come Together*, 261.

36 *The U.S. vs. John Lennon.*

36–37 Geoffrey Giuliano and Brenda Giuliano, *The Lost Lennon Interviews* (Holbrook, MA: Adams Media Corp., 1996), 139.

37 *Imagine: John Lennon.*

39 Bresler, *Who Killed John Lennon?*, 196.

38 James Henke, *Lennon Legend: An Illustrated Life of John Lennon* (San Francisco: Chronicle Books, 2003), 49.

41 Bresler, *Who Killed John Lennon?*, 87.

42 Ibid., 86.

42 Ibid.

43 Ibid., 96.

43 Bresler, *Who Killed John Lennon?*, 85-86.

43 Jones, *Let Me Take You Down*, 97.

43 Ibid., 93.

44 Ibid., 96.

44 Ibid.

44 Ibid., 103.

44 James R. Gaines, "The Man Who Shot Lennon," *People*, February 23, 1987, 70.

44 Jones, *Let Me Take You Down*, 117.

45 MSNBC.com, "The Man Who Shot John Lennon," *Dateline*, November 18, 2005, http://www.msnbc.msn.com/id/10100809/ (January 3, 2010).

45 Gaines, "The Man Who Shot Lennon," 73.

46 Nash K. Burger, "Books of the Times," *New York Times*, July 16, 1951, http://www.nytimes.com/books/98/09/13/specials/salinger-rye02.html?_r=2&oref=slogin (September 14, 2010).

46 James Stern, "Aw, the World's a Crumby Place," *New York Times*, July 15, 1951, http://homepage.mac.com/mseffie/assignments/catcher/Crumby_Place.pdf (September 14, 2010).

47 Bresler, *Who Killed John Lennon?*, 87.

47 Jones, *Let Me Take You Down*, 123–124.

47 Gaines, "The Man Who Shot Lennon," 73.

48 Paul L. Montgomery, "Police Trace Tangled Path Leading to Lennon's Slaying at the Dakota," *New York Times*, December 10, 1980, http://select.nytimes.com/gst/abstract.html?res=F20717FB3F5512728DDDA90994DA415B8084F1D3&scp (September 14, 2010).

48 Gaines, "The Man Who Shot Lennon," 71.

49 Gordon N. Sakamoto, "Suspect Bought Weapon in a Honolulu Gun

Shop," *Sarasota Herald-Tribune*, December 10, 1980, http://news .google.com/newspapers?nid=17 55&dat=19801210&id=5MYyA AAAIBAJ&sjid=72cEAAAAIBAJ& pg=5395,5111057 (September 14, 2010).

49 James R. Gaines, "In the Shadows a Killer Waited," *People*, March 2, 1987, 52.

49 Bresler, *Who Killed John Lennon?*, 153–154.

51 Jones, *Let Me Take You Down*, 177.

51 Ibid., 176–177.

53 Bresler, *Who Killed John Lennon?*, 202.

56 Gaines, "In the Shadows a Killer Waited," 60.

57 Jones, *Let Me Take You Down*, 20.

57 Ibid.

58 Ibid., 22.

59 *Rolling Stone*, "Behind the Photo: John and Yoko," September 13, 2004, http://www.rollingstone .com/artists/yokoono/articles/ story/6478087/behind_the_photo _john_and_yoko (January 3, 2010).

59 MSNBC.com, "The Man Who Shot John Lennon."

59 Bresler, *Who Killed John Lennon?*, 196.

60 MSNBC.com, "The Man Who Shot John Lennon."

60–61 Jones, *Let Me Take You Down*, 83.

61 Bresler, *Who Killed John Lennon?*, 201–202.

61 Montgomery, "Police Trace Tangled Path."

62 Gaines, "The Man Who Shot Lennon," 60.

62 Corey Kilgannon, "Recalling the Night He Held Lennon's Still Heart," *New York Times*, December 8, 2005, http:// www.nytimes.com/2005/12/08/ nyregion/08lennon.html?_r=2 (September 14, 2010).

62 Ibid.

63 Ibid.

63 Coleman, *Lennon*, 683.

63 *Montreal Gazette*, "'Please Pray

for John' Say Yoko and Sean, 5," December 10, 1980, http://news .google.com/newspapers?id=02UxAA AAIBAJ&sjid=waQFAAAAIBAJ &pg=4964,4113478&dq (September 14, 2010).

65 Bresler, *Who Killed John Lennon?*, 258.

65–66 Ibid., 225–226.

68 Jones, *Let Me Take You Down*, 75.

70 Lee Salk, "Convicted Killer: Mark David Chapman," *Pittsburgh Press*, August 19, 1982, http://news .google.com/newspapers?nid =1144&dat=19820819&id=I7gdAA AAIBAJ&sjid=_18EAAAAIBAJ &pg=6872,924446 (September 14, 2010).

71 *Bulletin Journal*, "Killer's Wife Mourns Lennon, but Can Forgive Her Husband," December 9, 1980, http://news.google.com/newspapers ?id=GRcuAAAAIBAJ&sjid=mC4DAA AAIBAJ&pg=6711,5258007&hl=en (September 14, 2010).

71 Gaines, "The Man Who Shot Lennon," 59.

71 Dudley Clendinen, "Lennon Murder Suspect 'Different Person' to Father," *New York Times*, December 11, 1980, http://select.nytimes .com/gst/abstract.html?res=F70912 F83F5512728DDDA80994DA415B 8084F1D3 (September 14, 2010).

71–72 *Nashua Telegraph*, "Mark David Chapman Sentenced to 20 Years," August 25, 1981, http://news .google.com/newspapers?nid =2209&dat=19810825&id=tqsrAA AAIBAJ&sjid=Sf0FAAAAIBAJ &pg=3845,4909907 (September 14, 2010).

72 J. D. Salinger, *The Catcher in the Rye* (New York: Bantam Books, 1986), 173.

72 Bresler, *Who Killed John Lennon?*, 279.

72 Ibid.

72–73 *New York Times*, "In Opposing Parole, Ono Cites Safety," October 4, 2000, http://www.nytimes .com/2000/10/04/nyregion/in -opposing-parole-ono-cites-safety .html?partner=rssnyt&emc=rss

(September 14, 2010).

73 David M. Herszenhorn, "Mark David Chapman: Vanity and a Small Voice Made Him Do It," *New York Times*, October 15, 2000, http:// www.nytimes.com/2000/10/15/ weekinreview/word-for-word-mark -david-chapman-vanity-and-a -small-voice-made-him-do-it.html (September 14, 2010).

73–74 Ibid.

74 *New York Times*, "Lennon's Killer Is Denied Parole for the 6th Time," September 7, 2010, http:// www.nytimes.com/2010/09/08/ nyregion/08lennon.html? _r=1&scp=1&sq=mark%20 david%20chapman%20 parole&st=cse (September 14, 2010).

75 Jones, *Let Me Take You Down*, 73.

76 Geoffrey Giuliano, *Lennon in America* (New York: Cooper Square Press, 2000), 222.

75 Bresler, *Who Killed John Lennon?*, 94.

77 Barbara Walters, *Audition: A Memoir* (New York: Knopf, 2008), 464.

77 Herszenhorn, "Mark David Chapman."

77 Bresler, *Who Killed John Lennon?*, 298.

79 Coleman, *Lennon*, 685.

79 Jean Williams, "Artists Express Love, Respect, Gratefulness for Ex-Beatle," *Billboard*, December 20, 1980, 104.

79 Ibid.

79 Ibid.

79–80 Ibid.

81 Bresler, *Who Killed John Lennon?*, 269.

82 Ibid., 292.

84 *IceNews*, "Iceland Home of Shining Lennon Memorial," September 14, 2007, http://www.icenews.is/index .php/2007/09/14/iceland -home-of-shining-lennon-memorial/ (September 14, 2010).

84 Giuliano, *Lennon in America*, 224.

SELECTED **BIBLIOGRAPHY**

Baird, Julia, and Geoffrey Giuliano. *John Lennon: My Brother*. New York: Henry Holt and Company, 1988.

Bresler, Fenton. *Who Killed John Lennon?* New York: St. Martin's Press, 1989.

Coleman, Ray. *Lennon: The Definitive Biography*. New York: HarperPerennial, 1992.

Elliott, Anthony. *The Mourning of John Lennon*. Berkeley: University of California Press, 1999.

Giuliano, Geoffrey. *Lennon in America*. New York: Cooper Square Press, 2000.

Giuliano, Geoffrey, and Brenda Giuliano. *The Lost Lennon Interviews*. Holbrook, MA: Adams Media Corp., 1996.

Goldman, Albert. *The Lives of John Lennon*. New York: W. Morrow, 1988.

Green, John. *Dakota Days: The True Story of John Lennon's Final Years*. New York: St. Martin's Press, 1983.

Jones, Jack. *Let Me Take You Down: Inside the Mind of Mark David Chapman, the Man Who Killed John Lennon*. New York: Villard Books, 1992.

Kane, Larry. *Lennon Revealed*. Philadelphia: Running Press, 2005.

Lennon, Cynthia. *John*. New York: Crown, 2005.

Lennon, John. *In His Own Write*. New York: Simon and Schuster, 1964.

———. *Lennon Remembers*. New York: Verso, 2000.

———. *Skywriting by Word of Mouth*. New York: Harper & Row, 1986.

Life editors. *Remembering John Lennon: 25 Years Later*. New York: Life Books, 2005.

Norman, Philip. *Days in the Life: John Lennon Remembered*. London: Century, 1990.

———. *John Lennon: The Life*. New York: Ecco, 2008.

Ono, Yoko, ed. *Memories of John Lennon*. New York: HarperEntertainment, 2005.

Sauceda, James. *The Literary Lennon: A Comedy of Letters*. Ann Arbor, MI: Pierian Press, 1983.

Thomson, Elizabeth, and David Gutman, eds. *The Lennon Companion: Twenty-five Years of Comment*. Cambridge, MA: Da Capo Press, 2004.

Wiener, Jon. *Come Together: John Lennon in His Time*. Urbana: University of Illinois Press, 1991.

———. *Gimme Some Truth: The John Lennon FBI Files*. Berkeley: University of California Press, 1999.

FOR FURTHER INFORMATION

BOOKS

Anderson, Catherine Corley. *John F. Kennedy*. Minneapolis: Twenty-First Century Books, 2004.

Aronson, Marc. *Up Close: Robert F. Kennedy*. New York: Viking, 2007.

Caputo, Philip. *10,000 Days of Thunder: A History of the Vietnam War*. New York: Atheneum, 2005.

Finlayson, Reggie. *We Shall Overcome: The History of the American Civil Rights Movement*. Minneapolis: Twenty-First Century Books, 2003.

Lindop, Edmund. *America in the 1960s*. Minneapolis: Twenty-First Century Books, 2010.

Manheimer, Ann. *Martin Luther King Jr.: Dreaming of Equality*. Minneapolis: Twenty-First Century Books, 2005.

Ochester, Betsy. *Richard M. Nixon: America's 37th President*. New York: Children's Press, 2005.

Partridge, Elizabeth. *John Lennon: All I Want Is the Truth*. New York: Viking, 2005.

Richards, Marlee. *America in the 1970s*. Minneapolis: Twenty-First Century Books, 2010.

Roberts, Jeremy. *The Beatles*. Minneapolis: Twenty-First Century Books, 2011.

Salinger, J. D. *The Catcher in the Rye*. Boston: Little, Brown, 1951.

Sherman, Josepha. *The Cold War*. Minneapolis: Twenty-First Century Books, 2004.

Spitz, Bob. *Yeah, Yeah, Yeah! The Beatles, Beatlemania, and the Music That Changed the World*. New York: Little, Brown, 2007.

WEBSITES

Imagine Peace
http://imaginepeace.com/
This is Yoko Ono's site featuring news about her art as well as her peace activism. The website provides a glimpse of Lennon's second wife and her career. It also includes information about Lennon's artwork and about the Imagine Peace Tower, dedicated to Lennon's memory.

John Lennon: The Official Site
http://www.johnlennon.com/
This site presents a multimedia portrait of Lennon, including a written biography, videos, and photographs.

Paul McCartney
http://www.paulmccartney.com/
McCartney's official website offers an overview of his career since his days as a Beatle and Lennon's songwriting partner.

sean ono lennon [dot] com: for all things sean lennon
http://seanonolennon.com
This official website of Lennon's younger son presents information on Sean Lennon's artwork, music, and more.

The Sixties
http://www.pbs.org/opb/thesixties/
This PBS website explores the tumultuous decade during which Beatlemania swept the world. Topics include politics, pop culture, and more.

DISCOGRAPHY

For a sampling of John Lennon's musical work—with the Beatles, alone, and with Yoko—check out the following albums:

THE BEATLES
Abbey Road. 2009. (Remastered. Originally released 1969.) EMI. CD.

Please Please Me. 2009. (Remastered. Originally released 1963.) EMI. CD.

Sgt. Pepper's Lonely Hearts Club Band. 2009. (Remastered. Originally released 1967.) EMI. CD.

White Album. 2009. (Remastered. Originally released 1968.) EMI. CD.

JOHN LENNON
Imagine. 2010. (Remastered. Originally released 1971.) Capitol Records. CD.

Lennon Legend: The Very Best of John Lennon. 1998. Capitol Records. CD.

Plastic Ono Band. 2010. (Remastered. Originally released 1970.) Capitol Records. CD.

Rock 'n' Roll. 2010. (Remastered. Originally released 1975.) Capitol Records. CD.

JOHN LENNON AND YOKO ONO
Double Fantasy. 2000. (Extra tracks. Originally released 1980.) Capitol Records. CD.

Milk and Honey. 2010. (Remastered. Originally released 1984.) Capitol Records. CD.

FILMOGRAPHY

The Beatles Anthology. DVD. (Originally released 1995.) New York: Capitol, 2003. This documentary series comprises interviews, live performances, and other footage of the Beatles throughout their career as a band.

The Dick Cavett Show—John Lennon and Yoko Ono. DVD. Los Angeles: Shout! Factory 2005. These television interviews from 1971 and 1972 show John and Yoko at their most political, most outspoken, and most candid.

The 4 Complete Ed Sullivan Shows Starring the Beatles. DVD. New York: Universal Music, 2010. See the Beatles as most Americans first saw them, beginning with their historic television debut in 1964.

A Hard Day's Night. DVD. (Originally released 1964). New York: Miramax Films, 2000. The Beatles' first film, this movie is light, funny, and fast-paced.

Help! DVD. (Originally released 1965.) New York: Capitol, 2007. The follow-up film to *A Hard Day's Night*, this movie is even more fantastic and wild.

Imagine: John Lennon—Deluxe Edition. DVD. (Originally released 1988.) Burbank, CA: Warner Home Video, 2005. This documentary, made with Yoko's cooperation, pulls together a personal portrait of John using home video, interviews, and more.

The U.S. vs. John Lennon. DVD. Santa Monica, CA: Lions Gate Films, 2006. This documentary examines John's political activity and the U.S. government's surveillance of him, using interviews with figures from civil rights activist Bobby Seale to news anchor Walter Cronkite to former FBI bureau supervisor G. Gordon Liddy.

INDEX

Adlerberg, Herbert, 67
Attica Correctional Facility, 69, 72, 73, 75, 77

Beatles, the, 6, 20–21, 22; break up of, 24; early years, 14–16; on the *Ed Sullivan Show*, 18, 86; films of, 18, 86; music of, 17, 21, 22, 86; origins of name, 13, 14; popularity, 17–20; songs of, 82, 88, 89; stop performing live, 86
Bellevue Hospital Center, 68
Best, Pete, 14, 16
Blankenship, Jessica, 47, 48, 55
Bresler, Fenton, 76, 77

Carter, Jimmy, 27, 39; reaction to Lennon's death, 79
Castle Memorial Hospital, 49, 50–51, 87
Catcher in the Rye, The, 45, 46, 51, 54, 58, 72, 86, 87
Caulfield, Holden, 45, 46, 51, 54, 66, 72, 75
Cavern, the, 15, 17, 80, 83, 86
Central Park, 54, 81, 82–83, 87
Chapman, David, 41–42, 43, 70–72
Chapman, Diane, 41, 42–43, 50, 71
Chapman, Gloria, 50, 56, 71, 75, 87
Chapman, Mark David, 56, 87; assassinates Lennon, 60–63, 66, 87; birth of, 41, 86; childhood of, 41–43; final trip to New York, 56–58; imaginary world, 43–44, 70; marriage, 50, 87; mental health, 43–44, 48–49, 50–51, 65, 68–70, 71, 87; moves to Hawaii, 49, 87; obsession with John Lennon, 51; obsession with *The Catcher in the Rye*, 45, 51, 54–59, 66, 72, 75; parole hearings, 72–74, 87; plans to kill Lennon, 53–58; prison sentence, 72, 87; public's hatred of, 66, 74; reasons for assassination, 51, 75–77; relationship with father, 42, 43, 70; sentenced for murder, 71–72; teenage years, 43–47; violent urges, 51, 56, 59; work for the YMCA, 45–48
Cold War, 29, 31
Columbia High School, 44, 47

Cosell, Howard, 4–5, 63
Covenant College, 48, 87
Cox, Anthony, 24, 89
Cox, Kyoko, 24, 89
Cronkite, Walter, 5, 33
Cullen, Peter, 61–62

Dakota, the, 5, 51, 54, 55, 56, 58, 62, 76; and vigil for Lennon, 6, 80; scene of Lennon's assassination, 58, 60–61, 66
Double Fantasy, 26–27, 56, 59, 60, 61, 82, 87
Dylan, Bob, 27, 88

Ed Sullivan Show, 18, 86
Edwards, Dennis, 65, 71–72
Epstein, Brian, 15, 16, 20, 22, 86

Fawcett, Anthony, 51, 53
Federal Bureau of Investigation (FBI), 36
flower power, 33, 35
Fort Chaffee, Arkansas, 47–48, 49, 57, 87

"Give Peace a Chance," 23, 34
Goldstein, Naomi, 68, 69
Goresh, Paul, 60, 61

Hamburg, Germany, 14, 15–16, 20, 80
"Happy Xmas (War Is Over,)" 36
Hard Day's Night, A, 18, 86
Harrison, George, 13, 14, 20, 87, 88; death of, 83; joins Lennon's band, 13, 86, 88; reaction to Lennon's death, 79
Help!, 18, 86
Hendrix, Walter Newton, 41, 43

Imagine (album), 24, 87
"Imagine" (song), 38, 44, 83
Imagine Peace Tower, 83
Immigration and Naturalization Service (INS), 25, 36
In His Own Write, 20, 86

John Lennon: One Day at a Time, 51, 53

Kennedy, John F. (JFK), 32

Leibovitz, Annie, 58–59, 81
Lennon, Alfred, 9, 10, 26
Lennon, Cynthia, 24, 85; marriage to Lennon, 16, 22, 86
Lennon, John Charles Julian. *See* Lennon, Julian
Lennon, John Winston: assassination, 4–7, 60–63, 66, 87; birth of, 9; books by, 20, 86; childhood, 10–13; deportation case, 25–26, 87; drug use, 22, 25, 84, 88; and fame, 23; fans' reaction to death, 6–7, 80–81, 83; as a father, 26, 88; first marriage, 16, 22; forms the Quarrymen, 13; last day of life, 58–60; marriage to Ono, 23, 86; music collaborations with Ono, 22, 36, 60, 86; in New York, 24; personality, 10, 13, 20, 84; political activism, 23, 25, 33–35, 36, 86, 87; songs by, 23, 34, 36, 38, 44, 83, 88; as a visual artist, 11, 13
Lennon, Julia, 9, 10, 11, 16, 88; death of, 13, 86
Lennon, Julian, 24, 26, 63, 85, 86, 87, 88; birth of, 16, 88
Lennon, Sean Taro Ono, 5, 6, 26, 82, 85, 88; birth of, 26, 87; theory of father's murder, 76
Liverpool, England, 9, 10, 11, 15, 20, 80, 81–82, 83, 86, 88, 89; birthplace of the Beatles, 13, 16
Liverpool College of Art, 11, 86
Liverpool Institute, 13, 88
Lookout Mountain, Georgia, 48, 87
Lynn, Stephan G., 62–63

Marks, Jonathan, 67, 69–71
Martin, George, 16, 79
McCartney, Paul, 13, 14, 16, 24, 84, 89; joins Lennon's band, 13, 86, 89; reaction to Lennon's death, 79
Mendips, 10, 11
Mintz, Elliot, 24, 63
Moore, David, 47, 49, 57

Nixon, Richard, 34, 36, 38, 87

Ono, Yoko, 5, 6, 21–24, 26, 58–60, 61, 66, 72, 79, 82–83, 85, 87, 89; as an artist, 21, 89; marriage to Lennon, 86; music with Lennon, 22, 36, 60, 86; political activism, 23, 34–35, 36, 86, 87; previous marriages, 22, 89; reaction to Lennon's death, 63, 80, 81, 87; tension with the Beatles, 22

Perdomo, Jose, 66, 76
Plastic Ono Band, 22, 36, 86

Quarry Bank High School, 10, 13, 37, 86
Quarrymen, 13, 86, 88, 89

Rolling Stone, 58, 81
Roosevelt Hospital, 4, 5, 6, 62

Rubin, Jerry, 34, 36
Rundgren, Todd, 44, 57

Salinger, J. D., 45, 46, 86
Season of Glass, 81, 87
Sgt. Pepper's Lonely Hearts Club Band, 21, 86
Shea Stadium, 18–19, 86
Sinclair, John, 87
skiffle, 11–12, 86
Smith, George, 10, 11
Smith, Mimi, 9, 10–11, 88
Spiro, Steve, 61
Starr, Ringo, 89; joins the Beatles, 86, 89; reaction to Lennon's death, 79–80
Strawberry Fields, 82–83, 87
Sullivan, Allen, 70, 71

Twenty-sixth Amendment, 38

Unfinished Music No. 1: Two Virgins, 22, 86

Valotte, 85, 88
Vietnam War, 23, 25, 31–32, 33–34, 38, 39, 87

Waldorf Astoria, 54, 55
Watergate scandal, 38, 87
White Album, 22, 86
Who, the, 13, 22
Wildes, Leon, 25, 36
World War II, 9–10

YMCA, 45, 47–48, 49, 55, 56, 66, 87

ABOUT THE **AUTHOR**

Alison Marie Behnke is an author and editor of books for children and young adults, as well as a photographer. Her books include biographies such as *Jack Kerouac* and *Pope John Paul II* and social studies titles including *The Little Black Dress and Zoot Suits: Depression and Wartime Fashions from the 1930s to the 1950s*, *Kim Jong II's North Korea*, and *The Conquests of Alexander the Great*. She loves to read, write, and travel. She lives in Minneapolis.

PHOTO ACKNOWLEDGMENTS

The images in this book are used with the permission of: © Bettmann/CORBIS, pp. 5, 25, 31, 32, 34, 67, 68, 80; © AFP/Stringer/Getty Images, p. 6; © Pictorial Press Ltd./Alamy, p. 10; © Craig Roberts/Alamy, p. 11; © Interfoto/Alamy, p. 12; © Hulton Archive/Stringer/Getty Images, p. 14; © Evening Standard/Hulton Archive/Getty Images, p. 15; © Keystone Pictures USA/ZUMA Press, p. 16; © Keystone Pictures USA/Alamy, p. 17; © CBS Photo Archive/Getty Images, p. 18; © Michael Ochs Archives/Stringer/Getty Images, pp. 19, 27; © AFP/Getty Images, p. 23; © Three Lions/Stringer/Hulton Archives/Getty Images, p. 37; AP Photo, pp. 42, 50, 54 (top); © Martin Heitner/SuperStock, p. 44; AP Photo/Greg Lyuan, p. 48; © Chip East/Reuters/Landov, p. 54 (bottom); © Ted Kinsman/Photo Researchers, Inc., p. 55; © Evelyn Floret/Time & Life Pictures/Getty Images, p. 58; © NY Daily News Archive/Getty Images, p. 61; AP Photo/Mario Cabrera, p. 62; AP Photo/Bill Sikes, p. 73; © Eyevine/Redux, p. 74; © STF/AFP/Getty Images, p. 81; © Astrid Stawiarz/Getty Images, p. 82; © Arctic Images/Iconica/Getty Images, p. 83; © Wendell Teodoro/WireImage/Getty Images, p. 85.

Front Cover: © Vinnie Zuffante/Michael Ochs Archives/Getty Images.

Main body text set in Janson MT Std Regular 11/16. Typeface proved by Monotype Topography.